D1332125

How To Get To
The Top Of Google

Reviews of "How To Get To The Top of Google"

"This book is the Bible of SEO"

—Michael

"Useful, organised and to the point"

—Adam

"Follow this book and you will get results"

—Stephen

"Buy it! Full of vital tools to help any company"

—Kerri

"5/5: Excellent SEO Guidebook WITHOUT Fluff!"

—Dave

"Reading this book is a must for every business owner"

—Dani

"5.0 out of 5 stars This is the book Google should have published"

—R. Lee

"Great simple and clear approach to your digital marketing efforts"

—David

"Amazing book written in plain and simple language – I can tackle my SEO now"

—Rosie

"Whether you're a business owner, marketing director, or student... this is for you!"

—Norvin

"Best book on understanding how Google works and using it to your advantage"

—Crispin

"Perfect for beginners such as myself to start understanding SEO!"

—Mr Dewing

"Straight to the point and easy to apply information"

—Dan

"Fantastic explanation of SEO for business owners"

—Fred

"Best SEO book you'll ever read!!!! FACT"

—Jamie

"Knowledge in the book is priceless!"

—Indre

"It Works!"

—Chris

Reviews of Exposure Ninja's Free Website and Marketing Review

"You guys are simply AMAZING! The most detail oriented and useful review I've ever received. I just can't see myself working with any other agency. Thank you so much for this priceless review! I'm really looking forward to working with you guys!"

—Bethlehem

"Massively useful 'kick up the backside' review of our website. PPC and SEO are presented in very clear terms indeed, and constructively. Currently loving the language and skills these guys use!"

—Andrew

"Quick turnaround time and surprisingly in depth for a free video audit. Lots of quick, actionable tips while bringing some important long-term aims to the fore."

—Simon

"I requested a free website marketing review for Exposure Ninja – was not quite sure what I would receive. The results were outstanding. A very personal, professional review of our website highlighting some key areas for improvement. Very detailed and presented in a great, easy to follow and digestible manner."

—Rob

"Exposure Ninja have been incredibly helpful, understanding the support needed for the size of the business and budget limitations. Loads of great advice I could immediately put into place."

—Kizzy

"Get the website review done! Exposure Ninja literally exposed so many things I needed to improve my website. There's no obligation and many helpful suggestions provided. Thank you."

—Kate

"After buying the audio book 'How To Get On Top Of Google', I had a free website review which I found incredibly useful and honest. The fact that it was a video review allowed me to see visually and more clearly where we were going wrong and how we can improve. I really can't recommend them enough"

—Brenna

"A thoroughly professional company who get the results you are looking for. I had a free website review done by Bevan who did a fantastic job highlighting areas I could make great improvements to that would significantly improve my site & convert visitors.

How many other companies give you a 15min video & a complete list of ideas or requirements to improve your website for FREE???"

—Darrell

"Exceptional insights. Nick provided a very clear picture for areas of improvement regarding UX and CRO. Well done! Read their content, listen to the podcast, and do not hesitate to get your review!"

—Seth

"I have just had a new website completed by the team at Exposure Ninja and I have to say I am absolutely delighted!"

—Kim

"The video review was great. A human taking the time to review the site rather than just site scanners adds a great touch. Clear and concise actionable tasks to carry out."

—Adam

"Wow! Cannot believe how detailed the free review was. So much information given in the 30 minute video – these guys really know their stuff. Would 100% recommend getting a review to get a professional, objective view on your site. Thank you!"

—Jessica

"This was one of the most valuable strategy videos I've ever had! Fantastic job and incredibly thorough."

—Midori

"Clear, insightful and actionable website review"

—Katie

How To Get To The Top Of Google

The Plain English Guide To SEO

Written by

Tim Cameron-Kitchen

and

Exposure Ninja

Dedicated to all of the Ninjas at the Dojo.

Sign up for **FREE Lifetime Updates** for this book and a **FREE Review of your Website and Marketing**

https://exposureninja.com/google-book

Table of Contents

Introduction

This book has helped tens of thousands of business owners and marketing managers get to grips with search engine optimisation—SEO, or 'getting to the top of Google'.

When I wrote the first edition in late 2011, I had no idea it would become the bestseller it has, nor did I expect it to have the impact it did on the people and businesses who read and followed it. The strategies in this book have been responsible for some incredible success stories.

Throughout, I'll share the methods that I and the Ninjas at Exposure Ninja (the award-winning digital marketing agency I run) have used to help our clients transform their businesses. I do this not to boast "hey, look how good we are", but to show you what the application of these techniques can really do.

These methods have been field-tested on countless websites and because we know the numbers behind the successes, we can say with confidence how well they can work.

For example, the graph below shows the daily revenue for one B2C eCommerce business that we've worked with to implement the strategies in this book.

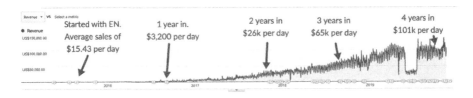

When we started working with them in 2015, their website was generating average daily sales of $15. By the end of 2019, we've brought that up to over $100k *per day*. Furthermore, the SEO and Content Marketing strategies you'll read about in this book are the only digital marketing that they use. This business has not used any paid ads.

(By the way, that drop in mid-2019? It was caused by a tracking error in the analytics code, not a drop in sales!)

Another client collects leads and sells them to solicitors firms. In just over 2 years, they increased their lead volume from just 35 per month to a high of 400 *per day*. Again, purely using the strategies in this book. No paid ads, no social media, no cold calling, no email marketing. Just SEO.

This graph shows how their 6-monthly traffic grew 1,658% and lead volume grew 1,226%.

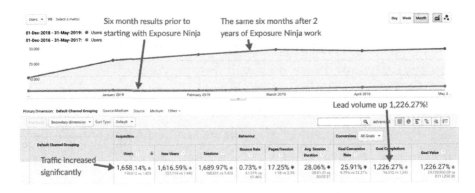

I'm not going to insult your intelligence with the whole "what would it mean to *you* to be 480X your weekly sales" routine – the impact of that sort of growth is pretty obvious. The reason I share these examples is to show what is possible when the steps in this book are followed.

The techniques in this book have helped startups go from zero to dominating their markets. They've helped SaaS companies find an audience for their products, eCommerce stores sell more products and service companies generate more leads than they know what to do with. They've also helped a whole lot of hard working entrepreneurs and marketing managers make a whole lot of money.

This book gives you a road map to increase the ranking of any website, wherever you are based and whatever market you are in. As most readers are doing this for profit, my ultimate aim with this book is to help you generate more leads and sales for your business.

As you'll read throughout, I've been doing this a while—first as a freelancer and then, since 2012, as the founder of a company I started called Exposure Ninja.

Exposure Ninja has grown to a team of over 100 due to the success of our clients, many of whom found us through this very book.

Back when I was a freelancer, building WordPress websites for tradesmen and musicians, getting to the top of Google was relatively easy. In some cases, I was ranking websites in top positions within 24 hours of them going live. One even hit the top spot *before it was officially launched.*

However, things have changed. Whilst the core principles of SEO are the same today as they always have been, the specific tactics have had to adapt. Google has become more complex and advanced and with more businesses relying on the internet for new custom, competition between websites is greater than ever.

Large swathes of the SEO industry have packed their bags, picked up their gold rush shovels and headed to the next 'land of infinite riches' (most of them are now running Facebook ads to sell Facebook ads training to people who want to get into selling Facebook ads training).

The thing that *hasn't* changed is customers going to Google to find what they want to buy. That's why getting to the top of Google is still right at the top of most business owners and marketing managers' wishlists and why actually achieving it is so financially rewarding.

Who this book is for and why it exists

This book exists to share what we've learned running SEO for hundreds of websites, whilst analysing the successes and failures of tens of thousands of others. It's here to lift back the curtain on the optimisation and promotion strategies that actually work, today, in the real world, and to show you how to implement these for your business in order to take your website traffic to a new level.

We share stories of the business transformations that have occured when these strategies are executed and explain step-by-step how you can take advantage of them in the same way.

The reality is that, stripped to their core, the fundamental principles of search engine optimisation are extremely simple. Whether you're an absolute beginner to SEO and digital marketing or you're an experienced SEO expert who wants to know the specific strategies we use for our clients, this book will give you the tools you need. Everything is explained in plain English and, where terminology is necessary, we've tried to give a clear definition.

As well as working on hundreds of client campaigns, since 2012 we've also been carrying out our world famous free website and SEO review for businesses around the world, and we've done thousands of them. Each time, we spend a minimum of 30 minutes analysing the website's performance, deconstructing its successes and failures, and measuring it up against competitors. As well as being a really valuable service for the businesses that request these reviews, it means that we've gathered a vast knowledge of what's working well out there.

> *After purchasing their Google ranking book, I submitted for a free website review. I can't believe how in depth the review was. A full 30 minute video explaining everything I needed to do, which was customised for me. I've scheduled a consultation with them to take actions on my website. Excellent service.*

—James

So whether you're B2B, B2C, B2E, DTC or any other possible acronym, whether you sell potato peelers, management consultancy, sexy massages or anything else imaginable or unimaginable; we've likely seen it, analysed it and ranked it, and the instructions in this book will help you sell more of them.

• • •

I wrote the first version of this book because I found that the clients I was talking to understood very little about SEO. Their knowledge had come from rumour, sales patter from unscrupulous companies, and online articles presenting baseless opinion as fact.

Many had wasted large amounts of time, money, or both, on ineffective SEO that was destined to fail from the start. If they'd only known the basics, they would have been able to see this. Hopefully, this guide proves as valuable to you as Amazon reviewer Ollie Chapman, who said, "Really useful book, I've managed to get on page one for multiple keywords in less than 6 weeks thanks to the tips in this book".

The first version of this book was a solo effort. This version is very much a team effort, with an assortment of our super high-calibre Ninja team contributing their individual areas of expertise.

I want to make it *absolutely clear* that without them, none of this would have been possible. They're inspiring, motivating, and they kick my ass on a daily basis. Charlie Marchant, Luke Nicholson, Dale Davies, Andy Tuxford, ex-Ninjas Rhys Herbert and Chris Groves, and designers Benz Alonzo and Andrei Shapa have all directly contributed.

However, the real work here has been done by the Ninjas at Exposure Ninja, working 'at the coalface' (or 'at the windfarm', if we're taking the climate crisis seriously) developing and refining the strategies you'll read about. Ninjas, thank you.

I hope you enjoy this book but I *really* hope that it helps you to grow your business and enjoy increased leads or sales through your website.

I would absolutely love to hear your success story or any questions that you have. You can email these to me at googlebook@exposureninja.com where the Ninja team and I will do our best to reply.

What sort of results can you expect?

The topics we'll be covering in this book broadly fall into two categories: what you will be doing to your website and what you will be doing elsewhere on the internet to promote your website.

If you find that a lot of changes to your website are needed, then you will usually start seeing results within a matter of weeks, certainly within a few months, after they are made.

There are some 'low-hanging fruit' suggestions that we provide for client websites (for example, optimising page titles, which we'll look at in Section 2), which can bring very quick ranking improvements.

Adding more text to a website that is mostly image-focused is another one of these low-hanging fruit opportunities to get some quick wins and to start noticing your ranking improve rapidly.

This graph shows the results for just such a business, a B2B eCommerce store.

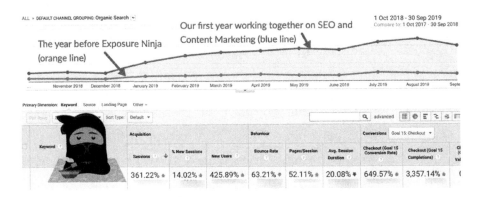

The top line shows their traffic during the period when they started working with us. Notice how things are relatively flat for the first two months before jumping up dramatically. Their sales went up 3,357% as a result.

In the example below, of a B2B client, the changes made to the website brought about the usual increase in traffic quite quickly, aside from the December dip due to Christmas.

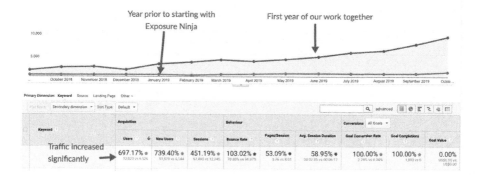

Once this website work is complete, you will need to move onto the promotion work discussed in Section 3. This promotion work is vital if you want to compete at the highest level or if you're in a very competitive market.

The strategies we'll share in Section 3 can be used to build market-leading visibility, even total dominance, and, as you'll see, they can produce game-changing results whether your business is brand new, already successful, or 'stuck' in no man's land. This type of work takes longer, however, and the results subsequently take longer to become visible.

One client that saw the majority of their growth from this work was a local business in London. Their website was well-designed and had already been optimised (the owner had read this book!). We worked with them to improve the site's ranking further by attracting local links and saw traffic increase 115% and online bookings 156% in six months.

Given that the competition in your market, your website, your current situation and the time you can invest can all greatly impact the speed of your results, I can't give you specific predictions about traffic and sales increases. This is why we've included lots of real life case studies in this book, so you can find businesses in a similar situation to yours and see what sort of results they achieved.

What being at the top of Google will mean for your business

In 2010, I was a professional drummer and was recording drums for people over the internet, which at the time was quite a novel concept. I built this business using SEO before I knew what SEO was, by copying what I could see the highest ranking sites were doing. One day, I was talking to my next door neighbour. He was a plasterer called Ben and I'd noticed that he was always in the house. I asked him how much business he was getting from the internet and he said "none". In fact, he didn't even have a website. This floored me, as my entire drumming business had been grown online, and I naively thought that this would be the same for everyone. I offered to build Ben a simple website and apply my fledgling Ninja skills to see if I could get it ranked on Google. I built it using a free WordPress theme, sprinkled some DIY SEO dust on it, and forgot about it.

A couple of months later, I had moved cities when I got a phone call from Ben. I still remember where I was when I took the call. He said, "Tim, it's the website. That website you've built for me... it's amazing". I was flattered, obviously, but also a bit confused. "The amount of work it's bringing me is amazing", Ben continued. I flipped open my surgically attached laptop and did a quick search. Sure enough, there was Ben's site at the top of Google for the phrase "Plasterer Tiverton", which was the town he was living in.

I was pretty pumped. It was a great result for a quick experiment and I hadn't expected it to work so well, or so quickly. The marketer in me kicked in, I grabbed my camera gear and set off on the two hour drive back to film an interview with him. I prepared a bunch of questions, as I knew how quiet Ben could be.

As I drove up to his house, I could see the front garden was strewn with plastering gear, covered in that white 'decorating dust'. I got out of the car as Ben was walking out of his front door. I asked him what all the gear was for and he explained that he was just loading everything up for a huge plastering job that he'd got from the website. I set up the camera, pressed record, and tried to remember my well-crafted interview questions. I needn't have bothered. As soon as the record light was on, Ben went off on one. The shy and retiring Ben was gone and he'd been replaced by a confident, full of energy and *very* enthusiastic Ben.

Ben explained that the website had been bringing in so much work that he was having to send out jobs to other plasterers, who were now working for him. He'd quickly become the "plastering kingpin" in town and had a part in most of the major jobs in the area. He then said that the success of the website had enabled him and his partner to think about buying a new house together, which floored me again.

This was my first taste of the impact that Google ranking could have on other people's businesses and I was instantly hooked. Since then, the Ninjas and I have been involved in lots of similarly incredible stories; clients becoming millionaires, starting businesses which gave them freedom from jobs they hate, dominating industries, taking on much larger competitors (and winning), and generally taking over their corners of the business world. This book contains everything that we have learned doing this.

Whilst each of the examples you read about will likely be in a different market to yours, the similarities between every campaign are far greater than the differences. As you'll read, the core principles are always the same and are actually extremely simple.

A free gift before we begin...

As a thank you for buying this book, I want to give you a jump-start on your way. Whilst this book gives you a clear path to follow to improve your website's ranking and sales, sometimes it's nice to have an expert show you two or three 'quick wins' that you can collect to get started on your journey.

I want to offer you a free expert review of your website and SEO, with some helpful pointers on the areas to focus your attention in order to start increasing your ranking and sales as soon as possible.

This expert review is not an automated software job. It'll be personally researched and recorded by one of our Marketing

Consultant Ninjas and sent to you as a video. The video will show you how to start making the improvements.

These reviews are genuinely fantastic and you can read feedback from very happy marketing managers and business owners on our Facebook page.

To get yours, go to https://exposureninja.com/google-book.

It's totally free and there's no catch. If you love the review, we'd really appreciate it if you told one person you know to request a review too.

How Easy is it to Rank?

One of the most exciting things about the internet, and Google in particular, is that it is supposed to offer a level playing field. Every business competes on the same Google results page, regardless of the company's size or age. When it works properly, consumers have a genuine choice.

I'm a firm believer that this is how it should be; a meritocracy with each player having the same chance to win. What it shouldn't be is an auction with a high entry fee, where the big players get bigger and the smaller fish starve to death.

There's a richness to search results that include recognisable brands alongside hidden gems and innovative, newer businesses. Audiences appreciate the speed and convenience of Amazon, for example, but that shouldn't mean that alternatives can't thrive as well. Boutiques, specialists and department stores can happily coexist online and consumers appreciate the choice.

So, how close does this ideal match with reality?

The days when websites 'accidentally' ranked highly are over. For any search with commercial intent, the top rankers are paying for that ranking, either through an SEO agency or through time spent doing it themselves. It's certainly possible for smaller sites to compete with the big players but they have to give the task its proper priority. Setting aside one day or £200 each month to compete directly with Amazon in the search results is like turning up to fight Sparta with a bucket on your head and a toothpick taped to a broom handle.

The key to competing, winning and dominating in this environment is choosing to fight the battles you know that you can win and prioritising this work. The great thing about SEO is that those who promote their websites most effectively will win, no matter their company size. However, those who think that they can outrank established competitors by clicking a few buttons every other Sunday or by paying cheapseo.biz or someone on Fiverr $200, will not.

We're here to help you with your online marketing by showing you everything you need to do to compete online, however large or small you are.

We've done this thousands of times in every imaginable market, and we'll lay it out, step-by-step, for you to copy.

How to Use this Book

There's no way around the fact that there is a lot of information in this book. Some of the tips, tricks and strategies in this book represent years of research and take many hours (even months or years) to implement. Others are quick and easy tricks you can do today to get fast results.

My advice is to cherry-pick the strategies that suit you. Do the ones that are most relevant to you and that fit in with the time you have available. However, please bear one thing in mind:

If spending a lot of time on a certain task turns you off, you are not alone. Your competitors are thinking exactly the same thing. That's why they're not doing it and that's why you should.

It boils down to how much you really want this and whether you are willing to invest the time and effort necessary. Hey, you're off to a good start – you're reading a book about SEO while they're reading fiction or watching celebrities eat animal genitals on TV!

I would recommend that you read about each and every strategy, whether you plan to implement it or not. It's helpful to know about the tools in your arsenal even if you don't intend to use them just yet. You'll start to spot these techniques in action and you may find yourself looking at the internet in a very different way! Prepare to become a geek.

If you are a freelance SEO or you run an SEO company, you'll want to know it all. Should you find yourself working with a client in a particularly competitive niche, it will be helpful to have some heavy firepower to back you up and give you the edge over the competition.

If you run a business and your competitors are employing a dedicated SEO company, you will be forced to do more work to compete (for advice on how to check what your competitors are up to, read on).

Please understand that just because a competitor might be employing an SEO company, it doesn't mean you can't still beat them. They are likely using the same, or simplified versions of, techniques you will learn about in this book.

With your specialist understanding of your market and your customers, you are actually in a competitive position. Remember – expensive doesn't necessarily mean good in the world of SEO, although it's a safe bet that cheap *does* usually mean bad!

The Structure of this Book

As the title of this book suggests, we will be focusing primarily on Google throughout and we'll start by understanding how Google really works. The good news is that the strategies in this book work just as well for other search engines, including Bing, DuckDuckGo, Yandex and Baidu.

It's widely accepted that Google works harder than any other search company to make its search engine is the most accurate and useful on the planet and its algorithms are by far the most sophisticated. In some markets, Bing is stealing ground but on the whole, anything that works to boost Google ranking is even *more* effective on Bing, so Google is where we'll focus our attention.

After understanding how Google works, we will take a look at your website and how to make it *Google friendly*, as well as visitor friendly.

Always remember that your website is built to generate customers, leads, or readers for your business. Never sacrifice *that* aim in order to achieve a decent Google ranking. Google is sophisticated and maintaining a prominent ranking won't happen if visitors to your website aren't having a good experience.

The third section of the book looks at promoting your website and building links through various forms of content marketing. This is absolutely crucial for high ranking and constitutes the majority of ongoing work that you will need to do in order to achieve and maintain top positions on Google.

Finally, we will look at piecing together a strategy for your website's Google dominance. You will see examples of Exposure Ninja's own strategies for getting websites to the top and, as always, you are encouraged to swipe at will and use for your own website.

For efficiency's sake, from now on, we'll assume that you are a business and the purpose of your website is to attract customers and make money. Whether you are an SEO company, SEO freelancer, or you run an information website or blog, the principles are exactly the same.

You'll also notice throughout that we mention certain resources to help you with your SEO. Most of the time, these are free, including website reviews, further information and handy software (for example, you can try Semrush [https://thankyouninjas.com] and SE Ranking [http://bestninjatool.com] for free via either link). The more entrepreneurial readers will take advantage of as many of these freebies as possible.

The Exposure Ninja free SEO and website review, for example, can save you weeks or even months of trial and error, showing you in 20 minutes what you might spend a year figuring out yourself. It's at https://exposureninja.com/google-book (if you haven't requested yours yet).

This Book is not Written by an Author

SHOCKING REVELATION! By now you had probably twigged that, whilst being eloquent, funny and *extremely* charming, I am not a professional author and neither are my fellow Ninjas who helped me write this book. Like them, I'm a professional digital marketer. We write how we talk and when choosing between 'easy to understand' and fancy language, we will always opt for the former.

Whilst our awesome editor has done what they can to polish our tur... writing, there will be times when eagle-eyed readers might notice a grammar or spelling error. If you want an SEO book written by someone who has no experience in SEO but has far superior writing skills, I have a lot of alternative books to recommend. However, if you want an SEO book written by people who know what they're talking about and spend their entire lives doing this, you're in the right place.

The end result is that we know what we're talking about. For me and the Ninjas at Exposure Ninja, ranking well on Google isn't a nice idea or a wish, it's a part of daily life and it's what feeds our families.

I don't say this to brag, I just want you to know that this stuff comes from testing, measuring and experience.

In this industry, there are so many self-proclaimed "experts" who have had little experience out on the front line. They cough up stories about strategies they've never implemented and offer opinions on topics they've only heard mentioned on forums.

Beware of the wizards. They're usually just cowboys in fancy dress.

Let's go!

SECTION 1

The Foundations

Whether you're brand new to SEO and digital marketing or you're an experienced pro, this section will explain the principles and terminology we'll be using and will give us a great foundation to work from in sections 2 and 3.

Most of the general public don't understand what it takes to rank prominently on Google, which is part of the reason it works so well. If they knew that the sites were ranked according to which website was best optimised and had the highest PageRank, they might dig a little deeper. Instead, many 'non-techies' assume that the top Google result is 'chosen' because it's the *best*. They place their trust in Google to serve them the *best* result. In general, it works out, and that has built a behavioural habit in the searcher.

The top result might have shoddy customer service, high prices and be run by the mob but Google doesn't care. Or rather, Google has no way to track this (yet). All Google does is run mathematical calculations (algorithms) based on thousands of different ranking factors and out pops an ordered list of websites:

Ranking Factors → Algorithm → Search Ranking

Change the factors, change the output. SEO is really that simple.

CHAPTER 1

Four free ways to appear on the first page of Google

People are sometimes surprised that there is more than one way to profit from prominent placement on a Google search page. In this section, we'll briefly touch on each way. Then, using the techniques in this book, you'll be able to increase your visibility in all of them.

Not all of these different types of results will show for every search. Google assesses the intention behind each search and will display the results it considers most appropriate, based on previous user behaviour.

Method 1: Google Organic Results

The 'normal' Google search results are the ones that appear running down the page with no 'ad' signs, as shown below.

The amount of traffic you get from your Google ranking obviously depends on the position you're reaching in this area.

According to Advanced Web Ranking's click-through rate study, ranking position one (top of Google), for example, can bring you 33% of all the clicks made by people searching for that phrase (down from 34.9% in 2020).

Ranking in position two brings only 15.99% of the searchers (down from 16.2% in 2020). By the time you get onto page two, even the top listing is only picking up a measly 1.03% of all searcher clicks (down from 1.86% in 2020).

You can see from this that the rewards for the top position are disproportionately high. It's just like the winner of the Olympic 100m race receives a disproportionate share of the rewards compared to the person who comes second, despite the runner up being the second fastest person alive.

One of the most common mistakes with SEO is complacency. Those running websites that rank on page one but not in the top spot, assume that there is little to gain by focusing on increasing their ranking further. You can see from these stats, however, that being persistent and aggressive until you own the top spot can really pay off.

Method 2: Featured Snippets

The second free way to appear on Google is through Featured Snippets. These are short pieces of text displayed by Google above all the other organic results on the page. As they're shown above all the regular results, they're often referred to as 'position zero' results.

The image below shows the search results for the question "what is Digital PR". You'll notice that, in addition to ranking in top position, the description from our website grabs a large amount of screen space, increasing the likelihood that a searcher will click to visit the Exposure Ninja website.

Method 3: Google Local

If you're a local business, you'll be well aware of Google's map listings that appear for searches likely to have 'local intent', as shown below.

As well as showing on the map, you can also have your business appear as a Knowledge Panel local result, as shown below (It's Ben! My first ever freelance client, seven years later).

Again, we'll look at how to encourage Google to show you in this area later in the book.

Method 4: Using Other People's Websites

Finally, it's worth mentioning that you don't have to use *your own* website to get business from Google. In fact, sometimes, appearing on a third party site can give you *more* credibility.

We have one client, for example, who picks up as many leads from an article we wrote on somebody else's website, as they do from their own traffic! This makes sense because if *someone else* writes about you and says how great you are, doesn't that hold more weight than if you're writing about *yourself* saying how great you are?

We'll look in detail at how you can exploit this opportunity when we cover sponsored content strategies in Section 3. Not only can it be a great credibility strategy but being featured on other people's websites is also a powerful tool for increasing your own website's ranking.

CHAPTER 2

How Google decides where to rank you and your competitors

You might have noticed that when we talk about "getting position zero" or "appearing in the map listings", or even "increasing your ranking on Google" in any way, we always say "we'll show you how to *encourage* Google to rank you here". Why encourage? Can't we just force our way to the top?

Folks who ask this are treating Google like a dog. You can discipline and train a dog and it will listen and obey, then your friends will give you admiration for your well-behaved fur baby. Google is more like a cat. You can try to discipline, you can try to train, but the cat won't obey you unless it perceives that it stands to gain big. Sometimes, even if it thinks it stands to gain, it will still just outright ignore you and rip its claws through your beautiful brand new sofa or wee on your shocked friend's brand new bag, just to prove it's the boss.

Therefore, when we're improving the ranking of a website or aiming for a position zero listing, the most we can ever do is *give Google what it needs in order to justify showing your website there*. We need to persuade Google that your website is by far the best and most logical choice for that piece of visibility. We need to make your website so perfect for the top spot that your absence would make the search results feel incomplete and broken.

Imagine, for example, that you Googled "online encyclopedia" and Wikipedia did not show up. You'd be thinking "what's up with Google?" You might even get super desperate and try Bing (bing.com, in case you need the URL). This is what Google doesn't want.

So, everything we do in SEO is about showing Google that your website *deserves* to be ranking at the top. If we do that, we crack the code.

The big question then is how does Google decide which website to rank first and which to rank second?

The answer is in the complex and secret algorithms it uses to measure and prioritise over 200 different ranking factors. No single person knows all of these and it's not possible, nor necessary, to master each one. Instead, we can break them down into three broad 'ranking pillars':

1. A website's relevance to the search
2. The popularity and authority of the website across the internet
3. The quality of the website

Let's look at each of them in turn.

Ranking Pillar 1: Relevance

More than anything, this is the word that defines Google's success to date. If the search results Google served weren't the most relevant in the business, this book would be called *How to Get to the Top of Lycos* because Google certainly wasn't the first search engine to market, or even the search engine with the best advertising. The reason Google is so dominant is because the results are more relevant, which means that web users *keep coming back.*

Google technologies like RankBrain, BERT and MUM get a lot of attention in the world of SEO, and with good reason.

RankBrain is a machine learning AI that helps Google to understand what we *really* mean when we search for things. When you search "Trump", are you expecting to see Top Trumps, news or background information about Donald Trump, or something else?

BERT helps Google's algorithms understand the context of words and to pick up on nuances that can alter the meaning of sentences.

MUM is "1,000 times more powerful than BERT", according to Google's update about its new AI improvement, which has a stronger grasp of language, so much so that it can find the answer to your query in another language and translate it for you immediately.

Why does any of this matter? Well, it matters because Google is obsessed with understanding what people are searching for and giving them exactly what they need. Any time you want to rank a website, you have to start by making it really, really useful and relevant to the search you're targeting.

How Does Google Measure Relevance?

Top of the list is the content on your website. That is the words and, to some extent, the pictures. Google has software, affectionately called 'robots', that are reading the internet constantly. These robots are crawling over your website and making a note every time each word appears. This process is called indexing. When someone carries out a search on Google, it runs through this index looking for instances of the words and coughs up the websites that those words appear on.

Straight away, you can see the importance of text if you're trying to improve your website ranking. If you're not using the words that you want to rank for, how could Google justify serving your website to searchers?

Myth Buster: Indexing

Indexing does not mean 'saving' your entire website, nor does Google store your whole website, but rather logging instances of particular words and phrases.

Google also doesn't index every single page it finds. There are a huge number of web pages online that get no visitors, which Google considers low-priority and doesn't bother indexing. It skips these pages because it prefers to prioritise the websites that it considers more important, namely those that are being updated and getting more traffic. The bad news is that if your pages aren't indexed, they aren't going to be showing up in the search results.

Now back to relevance. As well as the text content, another measure of relevance is *how searchers interact with your website*. Imagine you want to buy a new satchel. You go to Google and type "designer satchels". Up come the results, known as the search engine results page, or SERP.

From here, imagine that you interact with three different websites:

1. Firstly, you look through the Google results and see that one of the sites listed has an ambiguous description, which looks like it's not about designer satchels at all. There are lots of other more relevant sites though, so you click on one of the others instead.

2. When you land on this website, you have a brief glance and can see a lot of bags but few satchels and no *designer* satchels at all. You hit the 'back' button and return to the SERP.

3. You try clicking on another website. You land on a really useful page which shows that this store has a great range of designer satchels. You find a few you like, click between them, read some reviews and go through to make a purchase.

The billion dollar question is: *If you were Google, which of these three websites would you want to serve as the top result next time somebody searches for "designer satchels"?*

The answer, of course, is the third website.

Remember that the first website, the one that was ignored, was judged not relevant to the search. Over time, if a small percentage of the people searching "designer satchels" click on the first website, this low click-through rate (or CTR) will harm that site's ranking. Effectively, searchers are 'downvoting' it each time they ignore it and choose another website.

The second website attracted the searcher's click but failed to keep their attention. If this becomes a common problem for the website, this behaviour (known as 'bouncing back to SERP') will harm the website's ranking.

The third website attracted the searcher's click, kept their attention and resulted in a sale. Not only did this business make money but if this engagement happens frequently, Google will notice that people who visit that website don't come back to run the same search again. In other words, when they go to this website, they *find what they were looking for*. This site will eventually enjoy an increase in ranking. This will obviously increase their traffic and sales will rise. It's a positive feedback loop that results in more visibility, more traffic and more profit.

Ranking Pillar 2: Popularity and Authority

Another method that Google uses to decide where to rank any website is the site's authority and popularity. To explain how popularity and authority are measured by Google, I'm going to use a rather basic and sloppy term that I usually despise. It's quite useful in this situation, though, so for the next few paragraphs we're going to set aside SEO snobbery and discuss 'link juice'.

Link juice (also referred to as link equity) represents the secret sauce that Google uses to measure the relative popularity and authority of all the pages on the internet. To illustrate how this measurement works, imagine this situation...

Due to a strange set of circumstances, you have to recommend a restaurant to your in-laws, in a town that you've never been to. If you make a good recommendation, they will love and approve of you forever. Make a bad recommendation and you're struck off their Christmas card list for good. The stakes couldn't be higher.

How would you go about drawing up your list of recommended restaurants? Remember, you've never been to any of them and you don't know the town yourself.

You might ask your friends from this town which restaurants *they* would recommend. Over time, you'd probably notice that some recommendations kept coming up again and again. You might even keep a tally of these votes. This would start to give you a bit of a league table and the more votes a restaurant got, the greater the likelihood that it would be a solid recommendation.

With all the data on the number of recommendations, you would now be in a position to build a fairly reliable league table of the restaurants in this town. This would be a rudimentary ranking algorithm. You could build your own ranking algorithm which orders the recommendations by the likelihood that your contact would like them.

This is exactly what Google seeks to do. Its link juice algorithm measures not word-of-mouth recommendations but the virtual equivalent, the *links* to each website. Google's measure of each website's authority is called PageRank.

If lots of websites link to webpage A but no websites link to webpage B, then webpage A would usually be more popular and would have a higher PageRank. All those links mean that it's probably a more useful and popular webpage so, if all else was equal, it should rank higher on Google.

(Fun fact: the 'Page' in PageRank has nothing to do with web*pages*. It's named after Larry Page, the total supergeek Google co-founder who thought up the mathematical algorithm to measure it.)

However, it's not just the *number* of links pointing at a website that determines its page value. It's also the *quality* (i.e. the PageRank) of the websites that these links come from.

This makes total sense if we return to our restaurant recommendation example.

Rather than just relying on the *number* of recommendations for each restaurant, you might weigh the votes from your most experienced 'foodie' friends high. After all, if they regularly eat out, you could consider them an authority on restaurants, so it's only right that their votes are considered more influential. If your in-laws love Thai food, you might also give more weight to the votes of people who regularly eat Thai food because that would also make their vote more relevant.

Taking the 'authority' and 'topical expertise' of each vote into consideration, you could increase the likelihood of finding a restaurant that your in-laws love.

Let's look at an equivalent website example:

My website gets a link from a spammy blog comment on www.terriblespamz.biz, which is a trash site that gets no visitors. Meanwhile, your website gets a link from the Harvard University homepage (.edu website addresses hold particular weight with Google because they are less susceptible to being taken over by spammers). Which link *means* more? Which is a more reliable 'vote' on the quality of our websites? Obviously the link from a big-authority institution holds far more weight.

This would be reflected in the PageRank that our websites get from the links. Your website would get more PageRank from the Harvard link while mine would get very little from the spammy blog comment.

PageRank 'flows' through the links, so the Harvard website, which itself has high PageRank because so many other websites link to it, would *pass* PageRank on to your webpage. The low-quality blog that linked to my site, however, would have much lower PageRank as no-one links to rubbish websites, so would have less to pass on.

Note that, just like head lice spreading through a primary school, passing PageRank to another website through a link doesn't mean that your site *loses* PageRank by linking to it. PageRank is not a zero sum game and there's plenty to go around.

One final quick thing: the PageRank that a webpage passes on is shared between *all* of the outbound links on that page. Generally, the higher up the page the link appears, the more PageRank the linked page receives.

For example, let's say that your webpage was the single link from the Harvard homepage. In this highly unlikely example, your site would receive a *tonne* of PageRank. Imagine Harvard saying, "This webpage is the real deal. You have *got* to see this. Forget about everything else, just check out *this*."

If, on the other hand, there were hundreds of links on the Harvard homepage and yours was only one of them, the PageRank that gets passed along would be shared out by all the links on that page.

The only way to *create* PageRank is to create a new page. Each page is born with it and shares this sweet nectar with all the pages that it links to.

This means that bigger websites with more pages naturally have the opportunity to get higher page value because all their pages link to each other and boost their authority.

We're going to be looking at why you should build lots of pages on your website, in an orderly and well-structured way, and what you should be filling them with shortly. For now, think of lots of pages in orbit around your homepage all feeding link juice to it.

Let's leave link juice and PageRank there. We'll briefly revisit them when we talk about links later on but remember for the time being that the authority of a page has a significant effect on where it shows up in the Google rankings. In Section 3, which is all about content marketing, we'll explain lots of ways to get other websites to link to you, thereby increasing your PageRank and your Google ranking.

Ranking Pillar 3: Quality

No discussion on Google ranking factors would be complete without a mention of quality. Due to Google's desire to serve searchers with the most valuable results, it's obvious that the 'quality' of your website will be important. In fact, it's so important that Google has very explicitly revealed what it considers to be a "high-quality" website, by publishing the internal guide it uses.

In Section 2, we'll take a look through Google's own quality guidelines so that you can make sure your website ticks all the right boxes. For now, here's a really useful question to ask about any website that you'd like to get to the top of Google:

'Does this website genuinely deserve to rank position one for this phrase?'

Whilst there are certainly things you can do to improve the ranking situation for undeserving websites, the time and effort that you'll use to do so is huge. Conversely, improving the *quality* of your website in a few key areas can often 'unlock' the ranking improvements that you've been working towards.

Let's now look at these key quality areas.

Upgrade 1: Your Website's Content

Websites with thin content, meaning low word count, poor quality writing or pages with little to no text at all, always struggle to rank. Improving and increasing content is often the fastest way to boost a struggling site's ranking. This makes sense because Google tries to match the needs of searchers with websites that meet those needs. Have you ever thought to yourself, "what I need right now is a poorly written website with incomplete information"?

People sometimes resist the recommendation to increase the amount of content on their website. They say things like, "I don't want to ruin the aesthetic of my site with text". That is the wrong perspective. Imagine shopping for a new armchair. You walk into the store, spot one that you like the look of and ask the sales assistant about it. To your surprise, the sales assistant only has one thing to say about the armchair, "This is a fabric armchair and it comes in a light grey chenille. How many would you like to buy?"

How authoritative would you consider that person on the topic of armchairs? How likely are you to buy the chair? This sales assistant could be the world's greatest armchair expert, they might have even *built* that particular chair with their bare hands. However, without further information your perception of them, the store, and even the chair is limited.

Yet, there are furniture eCommerce stores online today that are guilty of this *exact* crime.

In fact, there are eCommerce stores trying to sell every product that you can possibly imagine who think that one line of text and a couple of low-resolution photos for each product is going to be enough to motivate people to buy. Not only is it commercially crazy but it's also not going to help their ranking.

Remember that Google wants to reward websites that are experts in their fields and *know what they're talking about*. How can it tell if a website is an expert on their topic if there's very little information about the topic on the page?

We'll talk more about content quality later on, but for now it's also worth noting that Google has been investing heavily in its ability to fact-check content. If it wasn't already important that the information on your website is factually accurate, it definitely is now!

Google NYC released a detailed research paper in which it explained the process it uses to check the accuracy of any claim. It's very long and, to be honest, quite boring. Instead, we recorded a podcast episode where Exposure Ninja's Head of SEO Andy Tuxford explains the key takeaways. You can find it by searching "Exposure Ninja How Google Thinks" on any podcast platform.

Upgrade 2: Errors and Broken Links

If you clicked on a top search result and found that the website was full of errors and broken links, you'd be surprised, right? Likewise, if it took 20 seconds to load, you probably wouldn't wait around.

Good quality sites don't tend to have these types of issues, so it stands to reason that websites that *do* have these types of issues can't be particularly good quality. We'll talk more about technical issues in Section 2 but discovering that your website suffers from some killer technical problems is actually excellent news because it means that some relatively simple fixes can often move the needle for you.

Upgrade 3: Mobile Friendliness

Mobile friendliness is a given these days but there are different types of mobile website, each with their own set of SEO pitfalls. We'll look at them and navigate you through the choppy waters later on.

For now, if your website isn't mobile friendly, you need a plan in place to address this *today*. Make arrangements to get a new website or talk to your developer about adding mobile func-tionality to your existing website but, either way, you need to be catering for the 50%+ of internet users using their mobiles. The importance of this cannot be overstated.

Don't have a developer? Contact our team, and we'll let you know what your best options are.

CHAPTER 3

How to find and rank for the most profitable keywords

Before we set sail into website optimisation and fully embark on our SEO journey, we first need to establish your destination; which phrases do you want your website to rank for? Targeting the wrong phrases, known as keywords, is a fairly common mistake. The part that confuses most people is assuming that if one particular search term gets the most searches, it must be the best one to target.

In this section, we'll run through a version of the keyword research process that we use on our client campaigns. You can also watch a video of the process and download a free spreadsheet template. Just search YouTube for "keywords exposure ninja" to see the full video (and don't forget to hit "Subscribe" too!).

Step 1: Brainstorm keywords

Start by writing down the names for the core product/service(s) that your business sells. These keywords are the 'seed' keywords, the ones you immediately jump to when describing your business or products.

For example, core services and therefore our 'seed' keywords for Exposure Ninja are:

- SEO
- PPC
- Content Marketing
- Email Marketing
- Influencer Marketing
- Facebook Ads Management
- Website Development

Core services for an event planning company might be:

- Corporate Events
- Corporate Parties
- Weddings
- Product Launches
- Private Parties

Next, imagine yourself in the shoes of your potential target customer and consider which phrases you would use if you were looking for these products or services.

When searching for a business, a customer may not always know the search terms used. For example, customers of Exposure Ninja may not know the types of digital marketing services we offer. Instead, they might search for their problems or a more general keyword:

- How to get to the top of google
- How to increase my traffic

- How to increase my conversion rate
- Sell my product
- Sell products online
- Grow business online
- List of marketing services
- Online marketing company

Customers of the events company might be looking for things like:

- Event organisers
- Arrange corporate party
- Product launch planner
- etc.

At this stage, don't filter or second guess yourself, just let the ideas come out freely. This phase is intentionally non-scientific as we need a broad base of 'common sense' keywords to start from. There will be plenty of time for filtering later on.

If you're stuck or you're researching an unfamiliar market, find an online chat room or forum and spend some time reading the threads. We'll sometimes use Quora or Reddit to research keywords for clients as they can be a great source of 'natural language'. How do people explain their situation? What's the difference in the language between the most experienced posters and the newbies and which group does your business primarily serve? You'll want to match the language you use, and the keywords that you target, to your audience's experience level.

Aim for a minimum of 10 keywords in your rough starting list, although this is likely to be much longer if you sell a large range of products. If you sell a huge range of products, you have your work cut out for you, as each product category will have its own group of keywords. In this case, I'd recommend doing the keyword research in stages, starting with three or four of your most popular or most profitable product categories. Over time, you can add further categories until you have your entire catalogue covered and optimised.

Step 2: Download keywords from Search Console

If you already have a website, you can check Google Search Console for keywords that you're gaining traffic from or ranking for.

Log in to Search Console at https://search.google.com/search-console/about, select "Performance" then "Search Results". You should now see a graph which shows you how many visits to your website have come from Google's search results. Beneath the graph, a table will show you the search queries your website has appeared for in the search results. Many of these search queries will make good keywords to add to your list.

Step 3: Use Semrush to find keywords

The next step is to find out the other phrases you're ranking for. We use Semrush for this, which is a paid tool but we've negoti-ated a 30-day free trial for you at https://thankyouninjas.com, which is well worth using as it is a fantastic tool that can save a *lot* of time.

Inside Semrush, you can drop in any website address and see the keywords that it's ranking for:

The Keyword column shows the phrase that the site is ranking for. Pos is the position the site shows on Google – so position 1 is top of the first page, position 11 is top of page 2, etc. Volume is the number of times this phrase is searched each month.

You may well be surprised to see some of the keywords that your site is ranking for!

Pick out any that look like they're relevant to your products or services and add them to your keyword list.

Now is a good time to talk about keyword search volumes.

You might find that some of the phrases you'd really like to rank for have a low reported search volume in Semrush or some other keyword tool.

Whilst keyword search volume is an important consideration, you want to take it with a massive pinch of salt for two reasons:

1. None of these tools really know or report the **exact** search volume of any phrase. Every number in that Semrush table above is an estimate and some of them are estimates based on other estimates.

2. Even phrases with low search volumes are worth targeting when the traffic is an exact fit for your business. Who would you rather have visit your site, 10 people that want to buy the exact product you are selling, or 100 people that *sort of maybe* want something similar to what you're selling?

3. We've built successful companies by securing rankings for phrases that apparently have 'no search volume'. My number one rule of SEO is never to trust data before common sense, so if you know you should be targeting that phrase, get it on the list!

Step 4: Check competitor keywords

We'll be seeing how to unpick your competitors' keyword strategy shortly but, for now, take a look at their website and see what sort of language they are using to describe what they do. Are they using any phrases that you might want to include in your keywords? Don't assume that they've got it right and copy them blindly, though.

Also, check their rankings in Semrush. Are they ranking for any of the phrases *you'd* like to be ranking for?

Step 5: If you're a location-based business...

If you run a local business or target specific locations, you'll want to tack these onto your keywords to make sure the searches are relevant. Make a list of nearby areas, counties, cities, towns and postcodes that are part of the area your business operates within.

Check the search volume, CPC and competition for the areas in Semrush. Decide which areas offer the highest value and should be worked on first. Use these locations as a suffix and prefix to each of the keywords.

Step 6: Find your most profitable keywords

Now that you have a huge list of keywords, you may well have over 100, it's time to prioritise and sort them into a manageable list of 10-50. You might be thinking that's a wide range, and it is, but then there are readers who sell one product and others who sell thousands.

During this process, I'm going to assume that you're using Semrush, although any keyword research tool should have similar metrics (For example, we also use SE Ranking internally. You can try it for free for 21 days using this link: bestninjatool.com). To analyse the metrics of any keyword just stick it in the big box at the top and you'll get that keyword's data:

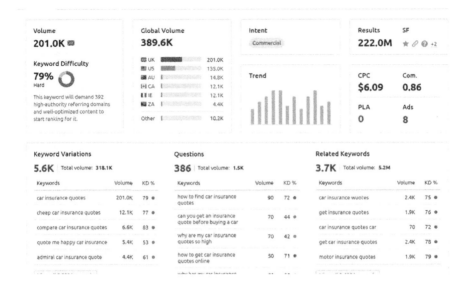

The Volume is an indication of how many people search that phrase per month. It's an *indication* because, as we mentioned earlier, Semrush doesn't actually know how many people search "car insurance quotes" each month. The CPC and Competition data are useful too and we'll explain how to use them shortly.

Bonus Tip: If your business is seasonal or trends driven you can use Google Trends (https://trends.google.com/trends) to see how interest in search terms has changed over the last year. It can often be worth targeting a keyword with low search volumes, if it's on an upwards trend, and stealing a march on your competition by dominating a valuable keyword before they even realise they should be going after it. Keep in mind that Google Trends shows relative data rather than actual volume, so the scale is always 0-100, with 0 being no interest in that keyword and 100 being the most interest that keyword has ever received.

As if you didn't already have enough keywords in your list, you'll see the Related Keywords section, which shows other similar keywords and Phrase Match Keywords, which show other keywords that *include* this keyword. You can click View full report on both of these tables to see the full lists. Again, add any that seem relevant to your keyword list as we begin to refine.

To narrow down your keyword list to your priority group, we have four criteria to use. The exact mixture and balance between each is non-scientific; there are no 'right' or 'wrong' keywords for your business so you have to use your judgement. Keyword research that is too heavily guided by either data or baseless opinion doesn't tend to be useful so I'd suggest getting all the information you can, then choosing the ones you consider best. We'll run through the criteria now and then go through some further selection and prioritisation tips:

Search volume: The search volume for your priority keywords should be high enough that there is enough potential to bring traffic.

Remember that ranking top for any single phrase is likely to bring you around 40% of the traffic from that search, so if your goal is to bring in 100 leads per month from a group of key-words with volumes in the 0-10 range, you know that you're going to need to rank well for a lot of keywords.

However, the key here is to find a balance. Keywords that have the highest search volumes also tend to have the highest level of competition, so if your site doesn't have great visibility yet, targeting the broadest phrases in the market means that you'll be waiting a long time to see your traffic increase.

Competition: This metric shows the level of competition in paid ads for this keyword, on a scale of 0-1, with 1 being the most competitive. High-competition phrases tend to have the highest *commercial intent*; if lots of advertisers are keen to bid on a phrase then it's usually because they're making money from it.

There's another competition metric in Semrush called KD, 'Keyword Difficulty'. This is an indication of the competition for the organic search positions and is scored from 0 to 100, with 100 being high competition.

As with all competition metrics, we have to again balance choosing phrases that we know we can win (low competition) with phrases that are worth fighting for (high competition). The phrases you choose to prioritise will depend on where you're at; if your site has low visibility compared to your competitors, then you'll want to start by targeting lower competition phrases. If you're already competitive, then gunning for the most competitive phrases in the market can be your goal.

CPC (Cost per Click): Like Paid Ads Competition, the CPC indicates how profitable the keyword is likely to be. The CPC is the average price that an advertiser pays for a click on an ad for this keyword. We use CPC to determine a keyword's commercial intent (how likely it is people are making purchases after making this search) because if advertisers are willing to spend a lot of money paying to advertise a phrase, it's likely that they're making money from that phrase.

For example, the keyword "short term loans" has a CPC of £10.90. This means that advertisers are willing to pay £10.90 per click for this keyword because the searcher is likely to have high commercial intent (they are looking for a loan) and the resulting sale is worth enough to the advertiser that bidding £10 per click is profitable.

The keyword "Aston Villa website" has a CPC of 28p. Advertisers are not willing to pay for clicks from these searchers because they believe these searches have low commercial intent, i.e. the searchers are not necessarily looking to buy something.

Step 7: Google keywords to check the search results are relevant

We always like to sanity check keywords by running a quick search to make sure that Google thinks the phrase means what *you* think it means. While many keywords may seem relevant, sometimes they have multiple meanings, aren't specific enough to your business, or can be interpreted by searchers in more than one way.

Is this search too broad to be relevant?

It's better to target niche phrases with low traffic and pick up all of those relevant searchers than to gain irrelevant traffic from broad keywords with higher but irrelevant searches. It can be tempting to go for super broad keywords that have really high volumes but you need to be cautious, as traffic quality and conversion rate tends to be lower the broader your keywords are.

Law firms, for example, may want to target "lawyer" or "law firm" but this search term can have multiple intents:

- Somebody wanting to know how to spell the word lawyer
- Somebody wanting to know what a lawyer does
- Somebody wanting to find an image of a lawyer
- Somebody wanting a type of law not offered by the client
- Somebody wishing to pursue a career in law
- Somebody looking for entertainment such as books or films about lawyers

A better solution would be a lower volume, narrower search term such as "criminal lawyer", "divorce lawyer", "personal injury lawyer", or "property lawyer".

For a business with very little initial visibility, you might want to go even more narrow, e.g. "divorce lawyer in Bristol", "low cost property lawyer", "no win no fee personal injury lawyer", or "local criminal lawyer".

Step 8: Now you've got your keywords, find your key pages

Key pages are pages on your website that you want to focus on driving traffic to and improving rankings. It's unlikely that your homepage will be the only page that picks up some juicy ranking and other pages on your site actually stand a better chance of ranking than your homepage for certain phrases.

Your individual service or product pages, for example, are likely to rank as they hopefully contain a lot of focused content about each of their specific topics.

In addition to your homepage and product or service pages, you might have blog posts or other content pages that rank particularly well and/or generate a lot of your traffic. These pages are also key pages as they are already contributing and, with a bit of additional optimisation or some extra links, can be pushed to contribute even more.

The quickest way to find these additional key pages is to use Google Search Console:

- Log in to Google Search Console: https://search.google.com/search-console/about
- In the left-side menu, select "Performance" then "Search Results"
- In the graph, check the boxes for "Total Clicks", "Total Impressions", "Average CTR" (clickthrough rate) and "Average Position"
- In the table beneath the graph, select "Pages"
- Make a note of pages and blog posts that have a high volume of clicks, impressions, clickthrough rate, and average position.

Make a note of these key pages within a spreadsheet. You'll want to map your target keywords to each page later.

If you have a large website, your list of key pages is likely to be long (more than 15-20). This is the time to prioritise so pick the ones that represent your top-selling product or service categories. Once these pages are ranking well, you can come back through this process with other key pages but, for now, we'll need to focus.

Next, we want to see what keywords these pages are currently ranking for, if any. To do this:

- Log into www.semrush.com (remember that you can get a free 30-day trial at https://thankyouninjas.com).
- Search your domain URL.
- Once on the domain overview page, scroll down to find the "Organic Research" widget. Find the "Top Organic Keywords" box within this widget and click the "View details" button.
- On the next page, click the "Pages" tab near the top of the page.
- This page will show you the pages on your website responsible for attracting the most organic traffic.
- You can click on the number of keywords in the "Keywords" column to view the keywords that each page is showing up for.

Next, you'll want to start mapping your keywords to your key pages, like so:

Key Page	Keyword Topic	Target Keywords

/boiler-repair	Boilers	Boiler repair, boiler breakdown, fix boiler, boiler engineer
Homepage	Plumbing & Heating	Plumber, heating engineer, boiler repair
/plumbing	Plumbing	Plumber, emergency plumber, local plumber

By the way, you can download a spreadsheet version of this table via this link: https://exposureninja.com/google-book-freebies.

The goal here is to map every single one of your priority keywords to a key page (or multiple key pages) on your website.

If any of your target keywords *don't* have a relevant key page, that's an indication that you'll need a new page to target these keywords.

Now it's time to analyse (and improve) your key pages...

For each of your key pages, answer the following questions:

- Does this key page mention each of its target keywords at least once?

- Are there more than 300 words of text on this page? Blog posts should aim for more. 500-1,000 words is a good start but feel free to go even longer if the topic justifies it.

- If a searcher using this keyword found this page, would they have their questions answered?
- Does the layout mean that the page is clearly relevant to each of the keywords, without the searcher having to dig or scroll around?
- Do the page headline and subheadings contain the target keywords or variations?

Chances are, your key pages could have more content, written in more depth, and use your target phrases more often. That's nearly always the case and a fast way to improve the ranking of your site.

One business that we've done this for is shown below:

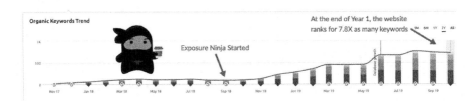

This graph shows the number of keywords that the site ranked for, over time. By building out the amount of content on the site's key pages, we were able to increase the number of keywords the website was ranking for by 7.8X, making them much more visible. In addition, because the content was better quality, we were able to increase the ranking for each of these keywords, resulting in an increase in leads of more than 30X.

A final word about keyword research

As you'll have noticed, keyword research is not an exact science and there are no right or wrong answers. You'll need to use your judgement and common sense because if you're looking for a tool or method to tell you conclusively which keywords you should be targeting, you'll be disappointed to find the only ones that will do this are too basic to be of any use.

Also remember that keyword research is never "done". We usually revisit our clients' target keyword lists every six months or so, once we've seen how the rankings responded to the optimisation, to make sure that the phrases we're targeting are still the most suitable.

CHAPTER 4

Analysing your competition and identifying their strengths and weaknesses

Now that you have your list of target keywords, it's time to analyse your competition.

When we're talking about SEO competitors, we don't necessarily mean *business* competitors but the websites you are up against in your target searches on Google. It's not unusual for a business to give us a list of their competitors and for us to find that, actually, the websites stealing all their traffic online are completely different to the 'real world competitors' whose names they have pinned to the office dartboard.

It's important to know who you're up against for a couple of reasons:

1. Savvy competitors can save you work by showing you what you should be doing. If you do more of what they do than them, you can win.

2. Less savvy competitors can highlight serious gaps in their approach, which you can exploit to leapfrog them.

Let's start right at the beginning. Go to Google and search for the one keyword you would most like to rank for.

PRO TIP: Checking Ranking

To check your website's ranking as seen by everyone else, make sure you're using your browser's Private Browsing or Incognito mode.

If you're signed into Google or Google Chrome, the search results Google serves you will have been tailored to your search and browsing history. If you visit your own website a lot, it'll show far higher for your searches than it would for a regular searcher, giving you a skewed impression of where you're really ranking.

If you've just realised that your site ranks a lot lower than you thought, I'm sorry, but you needed to know. You can also search using Semrush or another rank tracker, as this won't have the 'logged in biases' that a browser search might (try Semrush for free for 30 days via https://thankyouninjas.com).

For the purpose of this exercise, don't panic about where you show up in this ranking check. We're focusing on your competition here:

- Who is ranking well for this search? Are they direct competitors to your business? Is it large information sites like Wikipedia? If information sites, that's an indication that this phrase might be more 'informational' than 'commercial'. You'll need detailed content on your site to beat informational sites like Wikipedia.

- Are any of your competitors showing up more than once?
- Are there a lot of Google adverts for this keyword?
- Are any of your competitors using these adverts?
- Does Google suggest related searches at the bottom of the page? Should some of these searches be added to your keywords list?
- Are the sites that show up small businesses or large businesses?

If you are a local business, as well as the above, notice:

- Is a map showing up in the search results?
- If so, how many map results are showing up?
- Do the map listings have a lot of reviews?
- If competitors are showing up with only a few reviews, it can be an indication that they're 'accidentally' ranking for this phrase. Good news. If the listings have a lot of reviews, they're either extremely popular or, more likely, actively working hard to pick up those reviews. You'll need to be at the top of your game to beat them.

Once you've absorbed all the information from this page, choose another of your target keywords.

- Does the same competitor show up in the top position for this search?
- How many of the positions for this keyword are taken by competitors that showed up in the previous search?

- Are the same companies advertising as in the previous search?

To get the lay of the land, I usually repeat this exercise with three to five of my top keywords. The point of this is to really understand which companies are my main online competition for Google's top spots. If different competitors are coming top for each of the keywords, we'll want to study each of their strategies for each keyword.

If one website is consistently in first place for all the keywords, it usually means they really know what they're doing and have put a lot of work into this. I say *usually*, if it's a small niche or very local area it could just be pure luck or a hangover ranking from a time when it was easier to pick up visibility.

The next thing we will do is to choose three main online competitors from the sites that you've noticed rank well. Again, we're not necessarily talking about businesses that compete directly with yours but *search* competitors. They could be big chains, online retailers, or websites offering information.

If yours is a particularly profitable or competitive market, there will likely be more than three main competitors. If this is the case, pick the three biggest ones for now and write them down.

Of course, if your market is extremely uncompetitive or inhabited by technophobes, it might be the case that you don't actually have three competitors online. In which case, be thankful and write down as many as you have.

Deconstructing your Competitors' Success

We're now going to forensically study your competitors' websites and find out how they got to number one, so we can beat them.

Those readers who are uncomfortable with anything technical should skip to the next section if they find that they're struggling with any of the more geeky competitor snooping!

Pick your number one competitor and search for the keyword that makes them rank highest. We're going to have a look at exactly what shows up in the search results. Notice the title of their listing on Google; does it contain the keyword you searched for? Is the title of their listing short, or is it so long that Google has truncated it? You'll probably notice that their brand name is included in the title as well; is it shown at the start or end of the title?

Now look at the description underneath the title of their listing; how many times do the keywords show up in the description? Does it read like normal writing or is it broken up with ellipsis? Broken up descriptions tends to mean that Google has chosen to ignore the description provided, instead taking text from the website itself.

Notice what sort of titles and descriptions you can see on the page; do they entice you to click on the websites or do they sound boring and generic? If you were a customer, which would *you* click on and why? The Google results page contains a huge amount of information relevant to our mission so it's worth spending some time noticing which descriptions and titles stand out or make you want to click on the link. We can borrow from these enticing titles and descriptions later on when we're writing page titles and meta descriptions in Section 2.

Once you've made a mental note of your main target's description and titles in the results page, it's time to click on the link to their site.

Notice which page opens when you click on the link; is it the homepage (e.g. www.ninjasupplements.com) or is it a different page (e.g. www.ninjasupplements.com/protein-powders)?

On the sites with the best SEO, you'll notice that the address of the page that opens contains the keywords you searched for. In the example above, you'll see that the page ninjasupplements.com/protein-powders contains the words "protein" and "powders". This is good practice and we'll be looking at how to do this later on.

It also usually means that this page has been targeted specifically for the keywords "protein powders".

Next, we're going to have a look to see how many times the phrase you initially searched for shows up on your competitor's webpage.

Press CTRL+F if you're on a PC, or cmd+F if you're on a Mac to search the page content, and type in the phrase you searched for.

You'll see how many times the keywords have been used in the writing on the page. This number might be anything from zero, on very poorly SEO-optimised sites, to 30+ on heavily optimised or over-optimised sites. It will usually be somewhere in the middle. Does the phrase show up in the page's headline? In the menu? In the main content of the page?

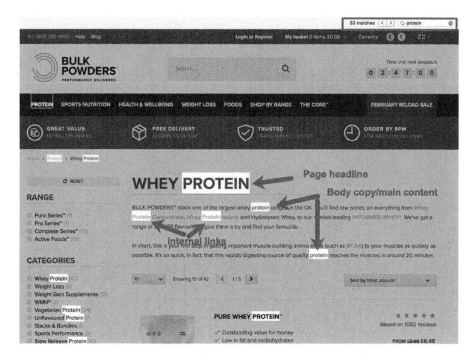

Next, find how many times the individual words in the phrase appear and also any variations, for example "roofer", "roofing", "roof". Google understands that they refer to the same thing and it's a good idea to include keyword variations on your page. Have your competitors used variations of the keywords in their text?

The next thing we are going to do is look under the hood of your competitor's site to see the optimisation they've used in the page's code, as sometimes they will have left telltale signs of their strategy which we can 'borrow'.

Right click on the side of the page, away from the text and picture content, and click View Source (also sometimes called View Page Source or similar).

The page's source code will open in a new window. We are looking for a couple of sections in particular:

The first section we're going to look at starts with <title>. What follows this <title> tag is the title of the page that showed up in the Google search. It's worth looking through this title to see how many times they have used the keyword you searched for and any variations.

If this title doesn't contain the keyword or phrase (perhaps it's just the company's brand name), it's good news because it's a strong indication that the site is not properly optimised.

This page title is one of the most fundamental and basic SEO elements on the website so if a competitor has their brand name on its own there, that's a total waste of an area that should be used for targeting keywords.

```
J)(winuow,uucument, scripc , uacaLayer , uim-i3yyiz/ i;</script>

<script type="text/javascript" src="//widget.trustpilot.com/bootstrap/v5/tp.

                                                                    tf-8" /><scripl
<title>Whey Protein | Protein Powder | BULK POWDERS</title>
                                                                    ks with Whey Pi
" />
<meta name="keywords" content="" />
<meta name="p:domain_verify" content="f56badefca2c46e9b10507b74e2af30d" />
<meta name="robots" content="INDEX,FOLLOW" />
<link rel="canonical" href="https://www.bulknowders.co.uk/protein/whey-prot
```

Now find the <meta name="description"> section, known as the meta description.

If you can't find it, again that can mean that the site is under-optimised, which is great news. However, for most websites that have been even slightly optimised, the <meta name="description" section will contain a brief description of the webpage.

This description is the suggested descriptive text for search engines to use in the search results, although Google will choose to display text from the page itself if it believes that it's more relevant to the search and content of the page.

This meta description can give us some valuable insight into the SEO techniques of your competitors because people tend to fill it with their target keywords as a summary of what they think their searchers are looking for, as well as with USPs that they think their customers find the most valuable.

```
<script type="text/javascript" src="//widget.trustpil

<meta http-equiv="Content-Type" content="text/html; c
<title>Whey Protein | Protein Powder | BULK POWDERS</
<meta name="description" content="Make delicious pro
/>
<meta name="keywords" content="" />
<meta name="p:domain_verify" content="f56badefca2c46e
<meta name="robots" content="INDEX,FOLLOW" />
<link rel="canonical" href="https://www.bulkpowders.c
<link rel="next" href="https://www.bulkpowders.co.uk/
```

```
<title>Whey Protein | Protein Powder | BULK POWDERS</title>
<meta name="description" content="Make delicious protein drinks with Whey Protein from BULK POWDERS. Shop for high quality protein powder and discover the UK's lowest prices.
<meta name="keywords" content="" />
<meta name="p:domain_verify" content="f56badefca2c46e9b10587b74e2af38d" />
```

The meta description in this example reads: "make delicious protein drinks with Whey Protein from BULK POWDERS). Shop for high quality protein powder and discover the UK's lowest prices." If you see some of your top competitors using low price as a selling point, unless you can compete on price, you might want to think about targeting niche versions of these keywords.

We'll be looking at meta descriptions in more detail later on but, for now, another indication of the level of optimisation of the site is the length of the meta descriptions on your competitors' pages. Google tends to truncate at around 155-160 characters so very long or short meta descriptions tend to be a symptom of an improperly optimised site. Google did flirt for a time with 260-character meta descriptions. The entire SEO world immediately started the mammoth task of updating every page. Google then changed it back. Hilarious.

The final piece we'll look for is a line that begins: <meta name="keywords"

If this line exists, the website owner has at least attempted to optimise their website to show up on Google. If you look further along the line, you'll see the list of keywords they have chosen to try to target.

It should be noted that this Meta Keywords field is totally useless; Google hasn't taken Meta Keywords seriously for over a decade.

Whilst you shouldn't assume that they have got the 'right' list, it can be really helpful to see which keywords your competitor has chosen, and there might be some that you haven't thought of. The point of all this research is just to absorb what your competitors are doing before we decide how and where to attack.

Close the source code and head back to the website.

It's generally good practice to have a separate page targeting each of your main keywords. This page will contain the keyword in the page title and the URL. The keyword should be found plenty of times within the text, plus variations and modifiers. Variations are obviously different forms of the same word e.g. roofer, roofing, roof. Modifiers are what we call 'add-on' words, so, for example, for the keyword 'roofer' one modifier might be 'emergency' as in 'emergency roofer'.

Try to notice whether your competitors have plenty of different pages all focused on different keywords or rely on a few pages to target lots of groups of keywords. Spend some time clicking through their navigation to see how many pages they have that appear to target specific keywords. They might not be linked to from the main navigation section so you might have to dig a little deeper to find them. If you can find a link to their sitemap to do this, great. If not, try going to: www.theirdomain.com/**sitemap.xml** or www.theirdomain.com/**sitemap_index.xml**.

You'll sometimes notice that these keyword-targeted pages are linked to from a section of links in or near the website's footer. The reason people do this is to avoid cluttering the layout of their website with links to dozens of pages, whilst still linking to them from every page. They effectively sweep them under the carpet and bury them at the bottom, out of sight. This technique is increasingly seen as just the wrong side of being spammy and while it's okay to have pages targeting different phrases, you always need to make sure that the linked pages are genuinely high quality and useful to visitors.

Now you are familiar with your competitor's website structure, keyword-targeted pages, behind-the-scenes optimisation and content, let's move on.

This might seem like a lot of work but trust me; this is a good way to avoid years of trial and error!

CHAPTER 5

An Introduction to backlinks

Remember that Google likes websites that have a lot of links pointing at them because this indicates that they're popular and authoritative. Popular and authoritative sites tend to rank better because they're usually better quality and more useful. So the next step in your SEO detective work is to analyse the number and quality of backlinks that your own and your competitors' sites have.

Google "Link Explorer", click on the tool and put in your website's address (you'll be instructed to create an account but don't worry, you get limited access for free).

This tool gives you an indication of how many backlinks your site has. It's not completely *exhaustive*, as Link Explorer doesn't index as many links as Google, but it's really useful to get an indication of the relative authority of different sites.

At the top of the Link Explorer page, you'll see a number of statistics:

- **Domain Authority:** This is an estimate of how authoritative Google may consider the website. The more inbound links from other high-authority sites that a site has, the higher the Domain Authority will be. We will discuss Domain authority later on in more detail.

- **Page Authority:** This is an estimate of the specific *page's* PageRank rather than the website's authority as a whole.
- **Linking Domains:** This section shows how many individual websites (root domains) are linking to your website

By putting your top competitors' sites in for comparison, you can begin to identify possible reasons as to why they might be outranking you. If you're being outranked, you'll usually find that your competitors have more links than you and, as a result, higher Domain and Page Authority.

Anchor Text

Within the same Link Explorer results page there's a section for Anchor Text.

Anchor text is the text used in a link. When you're surfing on the net, you might see an underlined word in blue, something like 'click here'.

Obviously, clicking on that link won't take you to a website called 'click here'. The words 'click here' are what we call the anchor text.

The reason that anchor text is important is because it's one of the measures Google uses to establish the topic of the linked page. For example, in the 'click here' case, Google would see the words 'click here' and associate the linked page with that phrase. If the anchor text was 'best protein supplements', what do you think would be on that linked page?

Hopefully, you can also see that using 'click here' as anchor text is not the best idea in the world.

A far better idea would be to use your keywords as anchor text, for example '_vintage furniture_' for a site that sells vintage furniture.

You can see the anchor texts your competitors are using by scanning the _Anchor Text_ table in Link Explorer. If you notice that they always have the same anchor text, take note, because this is likely the phrase they have singled out above all others to rank highly for.

It might seem like a good idea to create lots of links using your main keyword as the anchor text but this is where you have to start being careful. This strategy was used to death by low-quality SEO companies in the past, to the extent that Google actually started _penalising_ sites that used too much "exact match anchor text", where the anchor text _exactly matched_ the target keyword.

It's natural for websites to get a lot of links with their company name and website address as anchor text, so this is what Google expects to see in what we call a "natural-looking link profile".

If 80% of the inbound links say "_vintage furniture_" that starts to look a bit suspect. So when you're building links, it's a good idea to use descriptive anchor text, as long as you're being natural. We'll come back to links in Section 3.

For now, you should have a list of the keywords you plan to target and a list of your top competitors for those keywords.

You will have studied their websites, noticed the keywords they are targeting and how aggressively they are targeting them. You'll have observed the frequency of those keywords on the page, in links and in the meta description and <title> tags.

Phew! Next, we'll get your website optimised, Ninja-style.

SECTION 2

Your Website

CHAPTER 6

Website Optimisation

"Change begins at home"—IKEA

Any attempt to increase the ranking of a website needs to begin with the website itself. The best links in the world can't help an awful website, whereas a ruthlessly optimised site can take you a long way towards the ranking domination you might be aiming for, even before you start adding links. Aspects such as your website structure, the text on each page, optimisation of titles and meta tags and usability factors like speed and mobile friendliness all impact a website's ranking either positively or negatively. In many cases, they impact it significantly and quickly. Trying to promote a poorly-optimised website is like pushing water up a hill, whereas promoting a well-optimised website is like pouring it downhill.

The chapters in this section will show you how to make your website as 'Google friendly' as possible. We'll share the optimisation tactics that have unlocked significant ranking increases quickly and, in some cases, led to traffic growth within weeks.

Always remember the 10 million dollar question:

Does this website look like the sort of website that deserves to rank at the top of Google?

If your answer is no, then this section is particularly important.

First, some words about different website platforms:

I, along with many other people who like getting to the top of Google, use WordPress websites. WordPress is an awesome (and free!) platform that makes it dead easy to maintain your website. If you're starting your website building activities from scratch, 99 times out of 100 my advice would be to use WordPress*.

Having said that, it obviously depends on your needs. If you're building an eCommerce store, it might be best to build it using Shopify instead, which I'm a big fan of (as is our Website Development team) because it's really simple to use.

As well as being easy to use, Google really likes WordPress and finds WordPress sites very easy to read. Plugins (again, mostly free) enable you to add whatever functionality you like to a WordPress site without expensive development and by working with a professional designer and developer, you can be almost totally unconstrained by the layout you want for your site. In fact, pretty much the only time that we'd recommend a non-WordPress website would be for large eCommerce stores or custom platforms and even then, only when we're talking thousands of product lines.

If you're now really concerned that your website is *not* Wordpress, fear not. A well-built and well-optimised website will rank well on Google, *whatever* platform it's built on. We get a lot of emails along the lines of "My website is great and works really well, but it's not WordPress. Do I need to get it rebuilt in WordPress?" The answer is "absolutely not". Here are the only situations when we'd recommend considering getting any website rebuilt:

- You don't like your website. You will not push it as hard as you can if you don't actually *like* it. This is often overlooked, but important.

- Its conversion rate is extremely poor (i.e. it has traffic but brings you very few leads or sales).

- You've requested a free Exposure Ninja website and digital marketing review (https://exposureninja. com/google-book) and the recommendations aren't possible on this current website.

- You have little or no control over your website's contents, are unable to change the words on each page, or are unable to add blog posts without forking out a lot of cash. You will need to be doing this regularly, so it should cost you little to nothing or you might be disinclined to make the updates.

- It's not mobile-friendly and your developer quoted you an eye-watering amount to make it mobile-friendly.

- Your developer is the only one with 'the keys to the castle' and they suck (i.e. they are unresponsive or incompetent).

- Your website is heavily Flash-based. If so, kill it with fire immediately. It will never rank and Flash is being retired imminently. Old Wix websites fall into this category (new Wix is just about okay, just).

- Your CMS is no longer supported by the developer. We had a client recently who was forced to rebuild their entire website, purely because the development company that built it used their own custom platform. The development company went bust, stopped supporting the platform, and the client couldn't make important changes to the site. An otherwise usable website had to be scrapped totally.

Basically, you or someone on your team will need ongoing access to your website to make the changes required to get it to rank. If this access is expensive or difficult, it's time to consider a change.

There are three reasons we recommend using a Content Management System like WordPress for your website:

1. You will have greater control over the content on the site and will be able to update it more frequently, for example, by writing a blog, which will have huge benefits for SEO.

2. A lot of the on-page SEO we'll be covering in this book is much easier and quicker if you are using a CMS like WordPress.

3. If you want to change the look, feel or layout of your website later on, you can do this relatively simply and you won't have lost all your content or on-page SEO. You

can never fully 'future-proof' a website but this is as close as you can get.

If you'd like to know more about moving your site over to WordPress, just Google "exposure ninja moving over to Word-Press" to find a blog post I wrote to guide you through the overall process. Feel free to tweet me @timninjakitchen if you'd like a second opinion on whether a rebuild might be necessary.

CHAPTER 7

Domains and URLs

Your website's address or 'URL' can have a significant impact on its success, both from ranking and branding perspectives.

Addressing the ranking side of things first, before Google's 2012 Exact Match Domain update, it was ridiculously easy to rank websites using Exact Match Domains (EMDs) or website addresses that *exactly matched* what searchers were looking for.

For example, If you wanted to get to the top of Google for "flower shop nottingham" you could just set up www. flowershopnottingham.com and wait for the money to roll in. **I'm not joking.** We could rank sites within a day or two based *purely* on the domain in some cases, which meant we didn't have to worry about troublesome things like content and links.

Like all loopholes, this one was closed around the time of peak effectiveness. Having said that, many of the sites that ranked during this period are still enjoying top positions today, as the usage metrics are good and Google's algorithm has seen no reason to drop their rankings, despite EMDs no longer providing a benefit.

However, even *without* the EMD benefit, it can often make sense to use a more descriptive domain for your site.

If a fictional accounting firm called E Smith & Son, based in Bury, has the choice between www.accountantsbury.com and www.esmithandson.com, the more instantly descriptive domain name would be the first choice.

If a Google searcher types "accountants Bury", what is the keyword the searcher has in their heads as they look through the results for someone relevant? They're going to see a website address which exactly matches the keywords they're looking for and the website will clearly be relevant.

Key EMD Myths

Many businesses have, at some point, bought up large numbers of Exact Match Domains related to their industry. One of their first questions is; *"is there any benefit to pointing all of these domains at our main website?"* The answer is **no**.

The only way that these EMDs would be of use is if you were to build up separate, fully functional websites for each of them with unique, targeted content, thereby giving the site a high relevance for that phrase and then marketing each individual site to build its authority.

Great, but in the time it would take to do that, you could have turned your main website into an unstoppable mega beast by directing all resources at it instead.

Simply redirecting lots of new domains to your main site gives no SEO benefit either.

The second myth is that using an EMD actually *harms* your ranking.

People talk of Google's EMD algorithm update as a 'penalty' in the same way that other Google updates focused on links or website quality have penalised sites. Actually, the EMD update *removed some of the advantage* rather than installing a *disadvantage*. The perception of a 'penalty' only exists because sites that once enjoyed a significant benefit had this removed and they might have noticed a subsequent ranking drop.

Differences between TLDs

A common question is about the difference between different Top Level Domains (TLDs), for example, .com, .co.uk, .org and .ninja.

Should you go for a .com or a .co.uk? If they're taken, what about a .io?

As a rule, Google treats all TLDs equally (or so they say). In other words, a .com won't get you a ranking benefit over a .biz, despite a lot of spam/trash sites using .biz and other non-traditional TLDs. Alphabet, Google's parent company, even uses a .xyz domain itself.

However, that doesn't necessarily mean that you should use a fancy TLD because the .com and .co.uk are taken. Keep in mind that the general public is *extremely* unfamiliar with non-traditional TLDs, so could struggle to find or remember your URL. There's also a key perception difference between .com and something like .biz, which gives people the impression that it's second rate or that the .com has been taken.

In general, go for the domain name that gives you the biggest perceived authority in your space.

If you're trying to choose between the .com domain and your local country domain, the choice should be purely about what your audience is most likely to prefer. There is, to my knowledge, no clear evidence that says local TLDs outperform .com. For what it's worth, I'd personally always choose the .com when it's available.

Hyphens and Separators

As a rule, avoid the use of hyphens in your domain. As well as making them different to remember and tell people, they can be seen as a spam indicator.

However, hyphens in page URLs (e.g., www.ninjadresses. com/long-dresses/long-red-dresses) are fine and preferable to underscores. This is due to the way Google sees hyphens and underscores in URLs. Whilst Google recognises a hyphen as a word separator, it does not with underscores. So, long-dresses would be seen by Google as "long dresses" but long_dresses would be seen as "longdresses".

Domain Length

While we haven't seen any conclusive proof of a relationship between domain length and SEO friendliness, choosing a domain that is less than 14-16 characters long makes a lot of sense. Firstly, it's easier to remember and type correctly, resulting in less lost traffic as a result of misspelling. Secondly, long domains tend to cause problems in Google Ads because they can be too long to fit in the Display URL section of an ad.

Domain Age

The age of your domain *can* have an effect on your ranking, although Google's ex spam-fighting super Ninja Matt Cutts has publicly declared that the effect is minimal.

An older domain signals to Google that the website has been established for longer, so is therefore more likely to be a reputable business and less likely to use short term spammy tactics.

Secondly, websites tend to pick up links as they age, which can give older domains more authority than a brand new domain.

One myth is that the length of domain registration has an effect on ranking, i.e. if you pay for a five year registration when you buy your domain, your site will rank better than if you just pay for one year. The reasoning is that if you register your domain for the next five years, you must be planning to keep and promote the website for a long time and therefore be less likely to be a 'churn and burn' spammer, right?

While this makes logical sense, Google has confirmed this has no impact on ranking.

Capital Letters

Domain names are not case sensitive, e.g. ExposureNinja.com is identical to exposureninja.com. Even so, we recommend you keep all domain names lower case. Most internet users don't have this level of knowledge about how domains work and are used to seeing all lower case.

Page URLs

Using keywords in your URLs *does* have an SEO impact in the URLs of your pages. Imagine that you are a search engine trying to choose between these two pages to rank for "standard lamp":

- Page 1: www.bobslighting.com/d/1URvQqfaedz
- Page 2: www.bobslighting.com/lamps/standard-lamps

Which page appears more relevant for the phrase "standard lamp"? No contest, right?

Here's how that URL works:

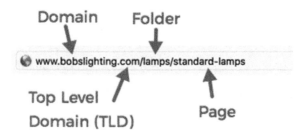

We'll cover the folder part in the next chapter when we look at how to structure a top ranking website but the page URL is the bit we are focusing on here ("standard-lamps"). The page URL should be short, descriptive and can use hyphens to separate words (it's rare that people need to remember specific page URLs so you're okay to use hyphens here).

How you set up your page URLs will depend on the website platform that you're using. Inside WordPress, for example, the first thing you need to do is check that your Permalinks are set to Post-Name:

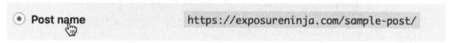

You'll then be able to set each page's URL while you're editing that page:

Once people realise that keywords included in their page URLs might help them improve their ranking, the tendency is to go all out and stuff every keyword they can possibly think of into their page URL:

ninjashoes.com/red-ninja-shoes-buy-ninja-shoes-online-ninja-slippers-shoes-sandals

This is not for you. You're better than that and 'keyword stuffing' isn't going to help you. It would more likely reduce the number of clicks the site gets from the search, which could actually *harm* your ranking.

No-one knows the exact measure Google uses to detect keyword stuffing in URLs so, in general, do what the highest quality websites do and use simple, short, descriptive URLs.

Capital Letters

Unlike domains, page URLs ARE case sensitive so exposure ninja.com/services and exposureninja.com/Services would be two different pages.

Using upper case characters can confuse your users and result in errors on your site if, for example, a user types in the wrong URL by not including the upper case character, or if you accidentally type the URL as entirely lower case in a link. Either of these will generate a 404 (page not found) error on your site, which is bad for user experience and can result in the user leaving your site and going elsewhere.

CHAPTER 8

How to structure a top-ranking website

Structure is important not only for improving your website's ranking but for helping visitors find their way around. Coming up are the internal Exposure Ninja structure guidelines that we use when we build websites for clients.

We tend to use bullet points to denote a website's structure. For example:

We would denote the pages that run along the top of the website as top-level bullet points, and the subpages as indented bullet points:

- Digital Marketing Services

- o Content Marketing
- o Conversion Rate Optimisation
- o Email Marketing
- o SEO
- o PPC
- Case Studies
- Training
  - o Guides
  - o Webinars
- Podcast

As an example, an eCommerce site selling Ninja clothing might have the following top-level pages:

- Homepage
- Clothing
- Accessories
- The Ninja Club
- Delivery & Returns
- About Us

These are all pages that general visitors to the Ninja clothing store website would be interested in. If a shopper wanted to browse for Ninja weapons, they'd go to *Accessories* and a drop-down menu would appear, which would include the *Weapons* category. There'd be no need to have a *Weapons* tab on the main menu because including every category would extend the menu beyond what is practical and could confuse visitors, like the example below:

An example of an over-cluttered eCommerce website menu

Think of your menu like the aisle signs in a supermarket; you don't want to put *every single* product on the aisle signs *but you want people who are looking for something in particular to know where they can find it.*

Whenever we're designing a website to rank highly, we start with writing out the top-level pages as bullet points. Next, we add our second-level pages as indented bullet points. Second-level pages are more specific and start to drill down into the products or services that you offer.

In eCommerce, second-level pages are usually category pages listing all the products of a particular type e.g. engagement rings or long sleeved t-shirts.

In the Ninja clothing store, there are a few different categories of clothing:

- Full Ninja suits
- Jackets
- Balaclavas
- Tabi boots

From our top-level *Accessories* page comes four second-level pages:

- Punching bags
- Weapons

- Headbands
- Bags

Next, we're going to add the third-level pages. These pages drill down into another level of detail. Not every website needs third-level pages but if you sell a wide variety of products or services adding them can help your customers (and search engines) quickly find the right category.

For our Ninja clothing store, I decide that punching bags is a second-level page that doesn't need another level of detail. However, after talking to my customers, I discover that they tend to be more likely to search for "Ninja star" or "Ninja staff" than the more general phrase "Ninja weapons". So, I decide to add another level of detail underneath the *Weapons* page by adding third-level pages:

- Shuriken
- Ninja stars
- Swords
- Nunchucks

...and so on.

At this stage, we're still not fleshing out the content of the pages but deciding on the overall structure of the site.

For local businesses that serve a number of different areas, it's a good idea to include pages targeting each local area.

Searchers tend to add locations to local searches, for example, "builders in Brixton" or "chinese restaurants CM2", so, by having locally targeted pages, you can begin to pick up some organic search results in addition to map results.

Let's look at an example. Harry's Home Extensions builds home extensions for people in and around Southampton, UK. As Southampton is quite a big city, residents looking for a builder to do their extension might be unlikely to search "home extensions Southampton". Some will, no doubt, but many more will use a smaller local area as the location modifier instead. Some of the areas within Southampton that Harry finds himself doing a lot of work in are Whiteley, Hedge End and Warsash, so he decides to make a separate page for each of these areas.

He calls these pages "Home Extensions Whiteley", "Home Extensions Hedge End" and "Home Extensions Warsash". On these pages, he describes some of the projects that his company has carried out, making sure to include local information such as the roads that the properties were on. He also lists some of the postcodes in the area and writes a unique overview of the service that his company offers, explaining why home-owners choose him to build their home extensions. By the time the website is finished, there are individual area-targeted pages with 400+ words of locally-targeted content, pictures from past jobs and some testimonials from people local to the area.

For a business like Home Extensions, optimising these pages and making sure they get indexed will likely be enough to have them rank top or very highly for their main target phrases. Not only this, but visitors landing on these pages have a higher chance of converting because the content is so relevant to them.

So whether you're an eCommerce site or not, these first, second and third-level pages mean that your audience can find really useful information collected in one place. From an SEO point of view, it means that you've got an entire page on your site targeted to a particular search, which gives you much better shot at ranking for it.

Yes, this means building quite a few pages for your website. Rejoice in the effort this takes because *this* is the effort that will set you apart from your competitors who don't invest in doing what it takes to get to the top of Google.

Folders and Directories

Your bullet point structure will need to be reflected, not only in your menu, but in your URLs too. We saw earlier how a particular page's address is made up of a folder component and a page URL component:

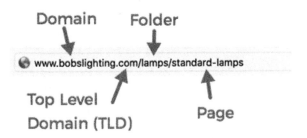

In this example, we can see that the Standard Lamps page is a 'child' of the Lamps category page. Using our bullet point system, we'd have something like:

- Homepage
- Lamps
  - o Standard Lamps
  - o Table Lamps
  - o Wall Lamps

It's important that the URL is presented like this because we're essentially telling Google that the Lamps page is the absolute daddy (or mummy) of all lamp-related subpages. All these other lamp pages are children of this Lamps page, therefore it must be super important for phrases around lamps. This increases its likelihood of ranking for broad "lamp" phrases.

We'll look further at optimisation of eCommerce category pages when we address content later in this section.

Use Separate Pages for each Service

This structure should also be used for lead generation or service business websites. If your business offers a service, there are likely to be various 'sub-services' that you offer as well. For example, an accountancy firm might offer accountancy but, alongside that, there might be tax returns, payroll, management accounts, auditing and so on. To simplify things, many businesses in this situation have a 'Services' page where they list the services they offer and write a couple of lines about each.

This is far from optimal, though. For a start, it's basically impossible to give someone enough information about what you do in a particular area in two sentences. Imagine a potential customer trying to understand a company's experience, USPs and the details of the required service in a couple of sentences! Secondly, by putting all of their services on a single page, these websites are hoping that Google will rank a single 'Services' page for keywords relating to every single service they offer. I've seen websites list ten different services on a single page. If we assume that each service has perhaps five target keywords, we're hoping that Google finds fifty different keywords relevant on this single page. That, Ninjas, is almost impossible.

The ideal approach is to have a separate page for each of the services you offer. That way, you can give visitors as much information as they need so that they can see you're a good choice *and* you can optimise each page for the specific key-words relating to the topic of that page.

CHAPTER 9

Sitemaps

Because websites can get pretty complicated when they contain lots of pages, it's a good idea to build a sitemap. This is a map of the website's page structure which we submit to Google, ensuring that its spiders are aware of every page on your website.

Without going into the details of creating your sitemap (if you're on WordPress, use any XML sitemap plugin such as *XML Sitemaps by Auctollo* plugin or the sitemap function inside *Yoast SEO*, and you're done), there are usually two types:

- XML
- HTML

XML sitemaps are designed purely for search engines. They contain code which tells Google how often it should recrawl the page and the relative significance of every page. As it's created for Google in XML format, it doesn't look very pretty and 'human friendly'. Note that just adding a page to your sitemap and submitting this sitemap to Google doesn't necessarily mean that Google will index that page. Google does what it likes and 'doesn't take no direction from nobody'. So the sitemap is just a friendly guide to help Google understand your website and find any pages it might have missed through crawling.

HTML sitemaps, on the other hand, *are* intended for human consumption. They are usually formatted in the same style as the rest of the website's pages and, because they're coded in HTML, they use a clearer layout which also indicates the page hierarchy.

Usually, an HTML sitemap is unnecessary unless the navigation of the website is so poor that visitors have to resort to scanning through a list of the site's pages to find the information they need. If you have an HTML sitemap on your website and you notice from your Google Analytics data that it's being used with any significant frequency, take this as a warning sign and rebuild your menus!

CHAPTER 10

One Website or Multiple?

Lots of local businesses ask about the feasibility of building multiple websites to target different locations. This used to be our standard advice when a basic site with an exact match domain name was all that was required to rank well. However, it's no longer so clear cut and, in most cases, promoting one *single* site across multiple locations can make a lot more sense.

Let's look at an example. A courier company with three city bases might have set up separate websites targeting each local office, using domains like www.courierliverpool.co.uk and www.couriermanchester.co.uk. All of the content on each of these websites could be locally-targeted, with branding kept consistent across all the sites. Nowadays, though, it makes more sense to create one awesome website with different pages targeting each local office (courier4you.co.uk/liverpool and courier4you.co.uk/manchester). That way, linking to and content boosting the authority of this one awesome site will benefit all of the individual locations, rather than having to raise the authority of a number of separate websites.

Therefore, the most common approach is to simply create new pages on the existing website, which are targeted at each of their locations. As well as saving time and effort, this approach has additional benefits:

1. The new pages are part of a well-established website, taking some benefit from existing PageRank, domain age and authority, whilst also making the existing website more authoritative because it has more content.

2. Being part of a larger website gives these pages more credibility, increasing conversion rate and sales.

3. Link-building and off-site promotion can be directed at just one domain rather than being split.

One case where we opted to combine a number of microsites was for a large global eCommerce store with eight separate country level microsites. The headache they had was optimising and promoting eight different websites and rewriting content for 750 products across each of these sites to avoid duplicate content. They also wanted to make each website multilingual, so would need to get each website's content translated separately. That's 750 products, written up eight different times, each being translated in four languages. Nightmare.

In this situation, we opted to amalgamate the local websites into one global website. This website automatically detects the country each visitor is in and shows them the local prices for the products and the local contact information as well as using their native language, although this can be switched. Each of the existing country specific domains were directed at the new website, making the visitor transition seamless. The team now has the far simpler task of keeping one website updated and the link-building work doesn't need to be spread across eight different websites.

Multiple microsites can still be a good option for businesses that have distinct customer groups or entirely separate products that don't share an audience. However, in most SEO cases these days, it makes sense to combine, rather than divide.

A dental client we have in Birmingham is an example of a time when having *separate* websites actually makes more sense. . As well as their dental practice, they also own a cosmetic enhancement clinic. In this case, we opted to keep the dentistry and cosmetic enhancement websites completely separate, as the dental practice was mainly targeted at families whilst the cosmetic clinic had a completely different target audience. In order to laser (no pun intended) target each website to their respective audience, the imagery, language and target keywords needed to be completely separate and the most effective way to do this was by having two distinct websites.

The obvious downside of this approach is that it involves a lot more work. Text needs to be completely rewritten for each of the sites to avoid duplicate content issues (covered later on), whilst the business has the job of maintaining and building links to two websites.

So, the decision to microsite or not to microsite really depends on the specific case. If it's possible to logically combine everything onto one website, that's the easiest and most efficient way to do it. However, if the customer groups are distinct or the messaging needs to be different, separate microsites can still be the best way to go.

CHAPTER 11

Website Usability and Performance

Much is made of website usability (UI or UX) as a ranking factor. There are tons of opinions online about how vital it is and even how UX *"is the new SEO"* (whatever that means).

So-called experts can talk about complicated UX designs until the cows come home but the important thing is that your website visitors find your website easy to use. Website visitors don't want to get lost in a labyrinth of irrelevant pages, they won't like websites that look spammy or have poor content and they certainly don't want to fill out ten pages of personal details before reaching the checkout. If you force that kind of experience on your website visitors, they'll leave your site and you'll have lost customers.

Google's interpretation of website usability is more restricted than the scaremongers would have you believe. Google can understand user behaviour by watching how searchers navigate to and from websites in search results; do they click on your website and immediately come back to search two seconds later, for example? It can also analyse websites using machine learning algorithms (including BERT and MUM). Finally, it can make judgments about the quality, and therefore the usability, of a website by looking at the link patterns and authority of the website. After all, no one links to a terrible website.

We've already looked at how Google measures behaviour of searchers and looks at links, so let's look at machine learning. In particular, how Google's algorithms use machine learning to judge the quality of your website. To do this, let me run through a little bit of SEO history.

In 2011, Google's Panda algorithm shook the low-quality spam world to its core. The algorithm was announced by Google like so:

"This update is designed to reduce rankings for low-quality sites—sites which are low-value add for users, copy content from other websites or sites that are just not very useful. At the same time, it will provide better rankings for high-quality sites—sites with original content and information such as research, in-depth reports, thoughtful analysis and so on."

The clues in this announcement are the general and ambiguous phrases "or sites that are just not very useful" and "and so on". How can an algorithm judge "sites that are just not very useful"? It can't. Or, at least, it *couldn't*.

You see, in order to develop an algorithm which *could* judge something as subjective as "quality", Google recruited human testers and gave them a set of 23 questions to answer about websites that they were shown on screen. These questions included, "Is this article written by an expert or enthusiast who knows the topic well, or is it more shallow in nature?" and "Would you be comfortable giving your credit card information to this site?" Working alongside these human testers was a machine learning algorithm which, given enough input about what the human testers considered good or bad, eventually learned to make the distinctions itself, creating an 'understanding' of what made a high-quality website. When the Panda algorithm was unleashed into the wild, pandemonium ensued. Google's search results saw an almost immediate improvement in quality and businesses that had relied on churning out crap in order to rank well were destroyed almost overnight.

You're probably wondering: *what is Google looking for when it's analysing how good my website is?'* The answer is that there is unlikely to be a single human alive who actually knows definitively. The next question, then, is, *'if nobody knows, how can we possibly make something that Google likes?'*

Remember that the algorithm is just aiming to mimic the *human* perception of quality, as measured by those 23 questions. If we build a website that performs favourably *for humans* answering the questions, we'll likely have something that the *algorithm* approves of too.

Here are the questions that Google asked its human testers to judge the quality of any website. As you go through these, it's worth asking yourself how well you think your website would stack up under this sort of scrutiny and what you could do to improve. If you make those changes, chances are, Google's quality algorithms will increase their perception of your site and your rankings will increase:

1. Would you trust the information presented in this article?

2. Is this article written by an expert or enthusiast who knows the topic well, or is it more shallow in nature?

3. Does the site have duplicate, overlapping, or redundant articles on the same or similar topics with slightly different keyword variations?

4. Would you be comfortable giving your credit card information to this site?

5. Does this article have spelling, stylistic, or factual errors?

6. Are the topics driven by genuine interests of readers of the site, or does the site generate content by attempting to guess what might rank well in search engines?

7. Does the article provide original content or information, original reporting, original research, or original analysis?

8. Does the page provide substantial value when compared to other pages in search results?

9. How much quality control is done on content?

10. Does the article describe both sides of a story?

11. Is the site a recognized authority on its topic?

12. Is the content mass-produced by or outsourced to a large number of creators, or spread across a large network of sites, so that individual pages or sites don't get as much attention or care?

13. Was the article edited well, or does it appear sloppy or hastily produced?

14. For a health related query, would you trust information from this site?

15. Would you recognize this site as an authoritative source when mentioned by name?

16. Does this article provide a complete or comprehensive description of the topic?

17. Does this article contain insightful analysis or interesting information that is beyond obvious?

18. Is this the sort of page you'd want to bookmark, share with a friend, or recommend?

19. Does this article have an excessive amount of ads that distract from or interfere with the main content?

20. Would you expect to see this article in a printed magazine, encyclopedia or book?

21. Are the articles short, unsubstantial, or otherwise lacking in helpful specifics?

22. Are the pages produced with great care and attention to detail vs. less attention to detail?

23. Would users complain when they see pages from this site?

You'll notice that some of these questions are subjective, whilst others are more objective. For example, "Does this article have spelling errors?" can be answered without dispute. "Is the site a recognized authority on its topic?" is much more open to interpretation and is therefore more likely to have a greater element of machine learning.

If you feel that either you're *unsure* how your site stacks up against these questions, or you know for sure that it's *definitely* missing the mark in at least a couple of areas, I'd suggest spending a couple of minutes looking at some of the websites that you spend the most time on each week. Whether they're news sites, blogs, magazines, whatever; how do *they* stack up?

Doing this a few times will help you to 'calibrate' your own machine learning algorithm (i.e. your brain) to notice what the key signals are that tell you, for instance, how much quality control is carried out on content. Once you're calibrated, revisit your own site and prepare to be horrified by the new insights you get.

CHAPTER 12

Mobile

Mobile Friendliness

Even a couple of years ago, having a 'mobile friendly' website was about making sure that it was basically functional on a phone; Did things fit on the screen properly? Did the website resize nicely? And so on. Since then, mobile traffic has increased so significantly that some of our clients' websites see more than 70% of their visitors using phones, rather than computers. Depending on your market, you'll likely be seeing 30-70% of your traffic coming from mobile too, with the number growing every quarter.

What this means is that mobile friendliness can't really be an 'additional feature' of your website, it needs to be fundamentally built in. At some point, most readers should really be going as far as to think of their entire business and online presence as 'mobile first', designing every page and interaction *first* for mobile and *then* working out what it needs to look like on computers.

Google's announcement at the tail end of 2016 that its algorithms would begin to rank websites primarily on what the *mobile* version of the website was like, signalled a fundamental change in how we, as website owners, had to view our mobile sites. In other words, if your mobile website was a dodgy add-on or a token 'plugin' version with stripped-down content and poor user experience, your ranking days were numbered.

So, how can you make sure that people's experience of your mobile website *helps* rather than *hinders* your ranking?

Responsive Websites vs Separate Mobile Websites

Back in the mobile internet ice age (let's just say pre-iPhone release in 2007), visitors on mobile weren't really a thing. Some geeks with BlackBerrys were trying their best but widespread adoption was a little way off. Even in 2012, only 10.7% of all website visits were from mobile. At this point, having a mobile-friendly website was a 'nice to have' feature; the cool folks at the country club would let you sit with them and your children obeyed your every word through sheer adoration and respect.

Most mobile sites at this point existed completely separately from the desktop versions and lived on a different URL (e.g. m.website.com). The mobile sites usually had dramatically stripped-down content and very little interaction. They often looked *terrible* but, hey, only 10.7% of traffic will ever see it. Who cares?

By 2015, s**t was getting real. Over 35% of website traffic was mobile, the folks in the country club weren't so chummy and your kids were starting to draw on the walls and show some dissent. That crummy mobile website that you had was seeing terrible usage metrics and, with 35% of your traffic now viewing it, you might have felt it was no longer up to scratch.

Most new websites from this point were built responsive, meaning they *responded* to the size of the viewing screen and adjusted their layout to suit a small, narrow viewing window. This is the default behaviour of most websites and, in general, is much preferred to having a separate mobile website. Here's why:

1. You only have one website to update. With a separate mobile site, each time you change some copy on your main site, you have to do the same on your mobile site. You already know you don't update your main site enough, so what are the chances you'll want to update *two* websites?

2. The mobile site doesn't lack any of the content from the main site. This is important now, as Google moves to the mobile-first index.

3. You don't have to worry about broken links, redirects and canonicalisation. Generally, life enjoyment is inversely proportional to the amount of time you have to spend thinking about these things. Having a responsive website rather than a separate mobile website will quite simply make you happier.

If your website *isn't* mobile friendly, or it technically is but the experience is poor, this is an absolute 'must fix', whatever you sell. If you need proof of that, then take note of the fact that mobile traffic is now 54.8% of *all global internet traffic (versus 50.1% in 2020)*. And if you want a second opinion, request a website and marketing review at https://exposureninja. com/google-book

CHAPTER 13

How to Write for Google and Profit

The role that your website text plays cannot be overstated. It's almost impossible to rank a website prominently unless the *content* on the website is *worthy* of that ranking.

We're sent websites to review on a daily basis from companies that have spent a small fortune on SEO, whilst failing to address the absolute basics of their website content. They have their foot hard on the accelerator pedal but their other foot is firmly on the brake.

At the same time, we get sent a lot of websites that appear to have taken the 'content = ranking' motto to the extreme, featuring an impenetrable wall of text in borderline invisible font size, explaining the same thing in 15 different ways using every keyword imaginable. The site's bounce rate is huge because visitors land on the page, vomit over their screens and run to competitors who can explain things far more simply and effectively.

In this section, we'll explain how to make your website's text worthy of totally dominating your market, without turning your website into a multi-page essay.

What is Good Content?

So what is 'good content'? Luckily, we don't have to guess. It's important enough that Google has given very clear guidelines about what it considers to be 'good'.

A high-quality website is considered to have "a satisfying amount of high-quality main content". This is not just generic, 'boilerplate' copy saying the same thing thirty different ways. Google's quality guidelines say that "creating high quality MC takes a significant amount of at least one of the following: time, effort, expertise, and talent/skill". MC stands for 'main content' or the main body of a page.

What this means in practice is that each page on your website needs to be detailed and authoritative on the topic it covers. Let's use an example:

A solicitors firm offers a range of family law services, from divorce to wills and probate. They have a single "services" page on their website, which lists the different services they offer and has a couple of lines of text about each. This is a common approach but, as we learnt earlier, it's nowhere near optimal if this website is going to rank well for competitive phrases. Each service (divorce, wills, probate) needs its own page and a good amount of text (we usually recommend at least 300 words) about what that service includes, how it works and what the visitor needs to do next.

This might sound like hard work—who can write 300 words about a divorce law service? Here's an approach that *you can* use to write authoritatively about *any* topic, we'll use the solicitor as an example:

Step 1: Describe what you are selling in detail. For example, *what does a divorce solicitor actually do?*

Step 2: Describe how it works, or the process that your clients or customers go through.

Step 3: Answer the top questions that people ask you about the product or service. For example, *how long does a divorce take?*

Step 4: Discuss why your clients or customers choose you, rather than your competitors.

Step 5: Answer the top objections that potential clients or customers might have about purchasing. For example, *will contacting a family lawyer make my divorce inevitable?*

Step 6: Describe the next step that someone should take to buy from you.

You can see from these simple questions that, actually, writing 300 words about each of your products or services could be relatively easy. What's more, we're not writing boring, irrelevant rubbish here either. We're actually writing stuff that people will *want* to read and that will make them more likely to buy the product once they have read.

Any time you're writing for your website, it's a good idea to use the language that your customers use. Call a spade a spade if your customers search for spades or call it an earth displacement device if that's what *they* call it. If your customers search for a range of phrases, then you'll want to make sure that you include all of those phrases throughout your text copy. Basically, imagine that your best salesperson was writing your website text. They would be friendly, personal, informative and extremely clear about what the next step should be.

Using your target keywords is important and you'll want to keep an SEO perspective on everything you write. Using keywords correctly in your text *is* important, despite some goody-two-shoes SEOs claiming that it's enough to simply "write naturally".

Let's go through the process of writing a website page from scratch.

The first step when you sit down to write for a particular page is to identify the specific keywords or phrases that this page is designed to represent. For our Ninja Clothing Store that we mentioned earlier, on the Clothing → Balaclavas page, we're going to write the text with the phrase "Ninja Balaclava" in mind as our *primary keyword*. This is the phrase that we would choose to get this page to the top of Google for.

A good starting point is to use your main keyword in the heading at the top of the page. If you are writing in HTML, put your keyword in the <h1> tags at the top (or set it as 'Heading 1' if you're using a user-friendly visual editor). This is a clear demonstration to Google that this phrase is particularly important to this page. As a rule, you'll only use one H1 heading on the page, so the fact that ours is going to be the phrase "Ninja Balaclavas" is a sign to Google that you're confident about the relevance of this phrase to the content of the page.

If you can do so without sounding too spammy, you can then use a variation of your keyword or phrase in an <h2> or 'Heading 2', underneath this main title.

For example:
<h1>Ninja Balaclavas</h1>
<h2>Buy Ninja headgear from the UK's Ninja balaclava specialists</h2>

You'll see we've used the word 'Ninja' three times (frequently, but not overused), 'balaclava' twice and there's one use of the word 'headgear'. Use of the word 'buy' tells Google and visitors this is a commercial site, suitable for commercial searches.

This type of heading and subheading really gets you off to a great start and it's a formula that you can use for every page.

If you are a local business, remember to include plenty of mentions of your location in all your website's pages. If you serve a number of different locations, mention them briefly on product or category pages, then link through to the specific targeted area pages we discussed above to enhance the local association.

A common mistake amongst sites struggling to rank is not being specific enough in their page headings.

For example, an accountancy practice will have at the top of its VAT accountancy page "VAT". That's not a useful heading because this page is not about VAT, it's about VAT *accounting*.

When a website is well-optimised, its service or product category pages can often outrank the homepage. This means that the people landing on these pages don't have *prior knowledge* of your business from the homepage content; they don't have a clue about what you do or who you are. So every page on your website needs to be capable of functioning like a landing page, introducing visitors to you and setting the scene.

Spelling and Grammar

The most sophisticated, machine-learning, search-ranking algorithm in history is analysing your website, looking for signals that it's either of a good quality or bad quality. Do you think spelling and grammar matter? I'll leave that there. If, like me, you have a tendency to misspell or type quicker than your brain works, Grammarly (www.grammarly.com) is a great app that checks the spelling and grammar of everything that you write, making you seem instantly more clever to everyone.

Another element to keep in mind is writing style. Google's Gary Illyes posted the following tweet in February 2017:

By "weigh less", he implies that the search algorithm shows preference for a natural writing style, which incidentally is almost the opposite of how most people "write for SEO".

Readability has long been a contested topic. Which sites rank better, those that are written in short, easy-to-read sentences, or those written in more complex sentences? My advice here is to write for the level your audience is at and, if in doubt, simplify.

We know that Google analyses reading level because until 2015 it allowed searchers to filter the search results by reading level. It has since dropped this feature, but it's unlikely that it dropped the underlying analysis and categorisation. So if your audience is likely to value easy-to-understand writing using plain English, cool. If your audience is technical and would be more at home with a more academic writing style, cool.

The Hemingway app (www.hemingwayapp.com) is a wicked app that makes sure your sentences aren't too convoluted to be understood, if you have a tendency to be quite technical and want to make sure that your writing still has mass appeal

Remember that Google's algorithms are designed to mimic human behaviour and preferences and they are getting better and better at this by the day.

Duplicate Content

It can be tempting to copy text between two or more pages. For example, if you have a lot of geographic areas that you serve and you want to write about the identical products and services you offer in each area, it might seem like a nice little shortcut to copy all the text and just replace the name of the area. Job done!

Unfortunately, websites that rely heavily on duplicate content don't tend to rank well. This makes sense when you think about it; how many of the world's best websites are likely to contain large portions of text copied from other websites or from other pages on their own website (unless you count Google scraping text to use in their search results, but that's an argument for a different day)?

The trouble is that 'duplicate content' has become known as a sort of SEO black plague. Many website owners are so terrified of inadvertently including duplicate content on their websites that they go through all types of bizarre gyrations.

The reality is that duplicate content is, to a certain extent, unavoidable. The text in your website's footer, the short product descriptions that show up in your eCommerce store in multiple product categories, and so on. Google has bigger fish to fry than to rip your site out of search results for these types of offences.

However, that's not to say that duplicate content is good or desirable. Both Google's John Mueller and Gary Illyes have confirmed that, although Google doesn't actively 'penalise' sites for having duplicate content, if pages on your site contain content lifted from other sites, they are unlikely to rank because Google will recognise that this is copied text and favour the source.

There is one situation where this type of duplication is extremely common and problematic and that's eCommerce.

If you run a store which uses the manufacturer's product descriptions on your product pages, these same descriptions are likely in use across dozens, hundreds, or even thousands of other websites. If Google sees thousands of websites using the same description, with many of them more authoritative and older than yours, what hope do you have of outranking them?

In cases like this, our recommendation is to write unique product descriptions *for each and every product*. Yes, this is a lot of work. However, if you need to get these pages ranking, it's worthwhile. Rewriting these product descriptions is also a good opportunity to add in some personality, maybe giving your take on the products as an expert who knows your market well. By doing this, you'll be providing additional value compared to the other 'me too' sites, and will justify better ranking as a result.

If you're unsure whether your website text might be duplicated, there's a super simple tool that you can use to tell. You can paste a web page URL, a list of pages, or even a block of text into Copyscape (www.copyscape.com) and it will show you how many websites are using this same text, along with the percentage of the page in question which matches your source.

Where a Site *can* be Penalised for Duplicate Content

There is one situation in which a website can find itself penalised and removed from search results as a result of duplicate content.

If Google's web spam team manually identifies that your site consists of a lot of content scraped together from other websites, rewritten slightly and with very little original thought added, they might decide that there's no need for Google to waste its resources crawling and indexing your site. This is rare though, requiring a manual penalty (it will show up in Google Search Console), so unless you're extremely unlucky, dumb, or both, this is not the sort of thing that would happen accidentally.

Headings

We touched briefly on headings and I want to spend some more time here as they are such an important thing to get right if your site is to maximise its ranking. Headings are the titles that you use on the pages of your website. They are denoted in your page's code by the HTML tags <h1> for Heading 1, <h2>

for Heading 2 and so on. It's best practice to use these heading tags in the following way:

- <h1> status is given to the page's main heading. There should only be one!
- <h2> is used for each of the main content sections on the page.
- <h3> is used for sub-sections or sections of secondary importance.

You'll set the H1, H2, H3 and all other headings in the code of your page. If you're using WordPress or a similar content management system, you'll see this dropdown:

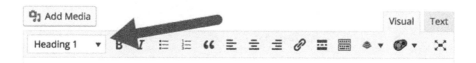

If you're using HTML, you'll need to code your headings like this:

```
<h1>This is a Heading 1</h1>
<h2>This is a Heading 2</h2>
<h2>This is a Heading 3</h3>
<p>You get the idea...</p>
```

Let's look at how some high-ranking sites use different types of headings:

INDEPENDENT   News   InFact   Politics   Voices   Indy/Life   Sport   Business

INDYBEST

Categories ⌄

Extras › IndyBest › Home & Garden › Lighting

10 best floor lamps   ⟵ H1

Illuminate your space with a stylish, standalone light

Riya Patel | Tuesday 12 December 2017 14.46 GMT | 💬 0 comments

0
shares

👍 Like   Click to follow
The Independent Online

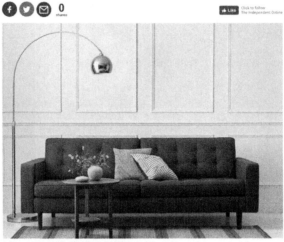

Could an over-reaching piece like this one from Heal's brighten up your day?

Winter's dark nights call for some extra illumination. A good lamp can transform an overlooked spot in your home into a cosy place of retreat. If you're keen to give a room some added warmth and atmosphere, a neutral lampshade or diffusing design is what to look for. Alternatively, a feature floor lamp can be just the thing to finish your perfectly-planned interior – one to dazzle guests with your sense of style.

On a practical note, think about whether the light needs to be adjustable, either by height or an angled head, or whether a compact lightweight lamp that's easy to move around will suit your space better.

Marks & Spencer Dexter Floor Lamp: £179, Marks & Spencer   ⟵ H2

INDY/BEST
BEST BUY
INDEPENDENT

This is a feature floor lamp with spherical shades that twist around a central stem. The polished brass finish and opaque shades gives the lamp a touch of glam. It would suit the dining or living room best, where it can be admired while entertaining. The base is heavy, keeping the slim lamp steady. It takes six G9 20W bulbs, which aren't included.

Buy now

READ MORE
- 10 best rocking chairs
- 10 best wall mirrors
- 10 best coat stands
- 10 best door stops and draught excluders

This information page ranks at the top of Google in the UK for the highly commercial phrase "best standard lamps" (at least, it did when I searched). It's basically a blog post containing the writer's pick of standing lamps, with some text for each one and a link through to the product page on the relevant manufacturer's website. Bizarrely, the site hasn't chosen to use affiliate links here, or it could be generating income through the recommendations, but that's another story.

The main headline of the page uses a H1 heading, it is short, and includes the article's target keyword ("best floor lamps"). The sections of the article, the products themselves, use H2 headings and include the target keyword again ("Marks & Spencer Dexter **Floor Lamp**").

Notice also that there is copy describing each lamp and why someone might want a standard lamp. It's not massively useful and you likely already know *why* you want a standard lamp but it needs to be there so that this article justifies ranking.

This next example is an eCommerce category page, which ranks for "standard lamps":

Notice that it follows a similar pattern; an H1 heading at the top of the page, using the target keyword, and H2s given to each main section of content, which, in this case, are the products. There's a block of body copy at the bottom of this category page, which uses an H3 heading. Again, the body copy is necessary to demonstrate the topic of the page and justify ranking. Without it, this page would have had a much harder time picking up the top ranking it has.

So, just by looking at the sites which are ranking well for some super competitive and highly commercial phrases, we can see how important the correct use of heading tags is. Go forth!

Content for eCommerce (or Other Large Websites)

If you're an eCommerce store owner with loads of products listed on your site, you might be wondering if you have to write copy for each and every single one of them. The good news is that you don't, only for the products that you want to get ranked and actually sell.

Standard product descriptions provided by manufacturers or distributors are usually no good here either because they're used on other websites and, as we saw earlier, that type of duplicate content is likely to be ignored by Google.

If your website has nothing unique to say about these products, how could Google justify ranking you above competitors saying the exact same things? This is a particular problem for 'ready made' affiliate or dropship sites, which are supplied 'finished'. Unfortunately, they're usually churned out duplicates with dozens or hundreds of identical copies, so are extremely unlikely to rank in their current state.

This obviously means a lot of work needs to be done when writing good quality content, so the key here is to prioritise.

How we tend to approach this for clients, and how I suggest you approach this yourself, is to prioritise the product categories that are most profitable, most popular, or that you have a head start in selling because, for example, you have a better range than your competitors in this particular category.

A client of ours sells protein supplements. In their online store are dozens of protein powders from some of the world's biggest names, each using the manufacturer-provided descriptions. This market is so saturated and price-driven that to get these products ranking would take a lot of time and money that the client didn't have. Instead, we took the decision to focus on a particular range of protein powders designed for a specific niche of their customers; crossfit fans. We identified the products that are most likely to appeal to crossfitters (all natural supplements, nothing artificial) and focused on this specific market.

By putting all our attention here rather than trying to spread it out across all the supplements they sell, the depth and relevance of the content is greater, these pages will be more likely to rank for crossfit-related phrases, and they'll be more likely to convert crossfitters when they *land* on these pages. The margin on these products can be higher because the audience perceives a much stronger match, and the website becomes more profitable. By doing this, you can take a website from being one of 10,000 sites competing for extremely competitive phrases, where little margin is available, and make it part of a smaller number of websites targeting a much more profitable and less cutthroat, price-driven market.

CHAPTER 14

How to use Knowledge Bases and FAQs to 10X your Organic Traffic

We've discussed how content is absolutely vital if you want to get your website ranking but many website owners struggle to get enough content on their product or service pages.

Something that we frequently do with clients is to create a Knowledge Base or a FAQ section. This is a content section that can be added to your website that covers your topic in detail and answers the most common questions. Not only is this a great way to demonstrate your expertise in your field but it's also a phenomenal way of increasing your traffic from Google.

Let's look at an example to illustrate.

SJD Accountancy is an accountancy firm that absolutely nails the Knowledge Base strategy. Here's their website:

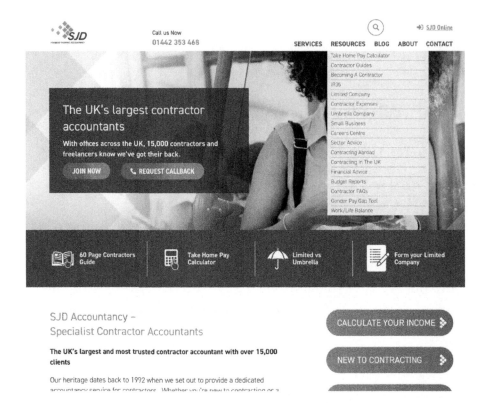

You'll be able to see from the highlighted Resources menu that they have a phenomenal amount of content on this website; guides for small businesses, contractors, an excellent range of calculator tools, and so on. So why have they bothered with all of this content, which must have taken a huge amount of time and/or money to put together?

Here's what Semrush estimates this website is pulling in:

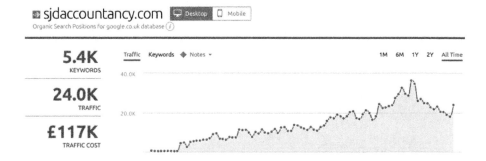

That's an estimated 24,000 visitors per month for an accountancy practice with an estimated equivalent value of £117k in Google Ads spend, per month.

Of course, these numbers are Semrush guesstimates based on their rankings, search volumes and advertising costs for the phrases that they're ranking for. Even so, this Knowledge Base might have cost them £40k to put together in time and energy (or outsourcing) but it should pay off for *years*.

Here are some of the phrases they're ranking for, which are expected to bring them the most traffic:

Organic Search Positions 1 - 100 (8,168) *i*

		Keyword	Pos. ⬍	Volume ⬍	CPC (GBP) ⬍	URL	Costs (GBP) ⬍
>	☐	contractor flat rate vat	1 → 1	70	5.98	https://www.sj... ide/ ⬈	196.4
>	☐	changes to ir35 public sector	1 → 1	50	0.00	https://www.sj... tor/ ⬈	0
>	☐	uk contractor services	1 → 1	90	0.00	https://www.sj... tor/ ⬈	0
>	☐	contractor pay	1 → 1	110	5.06	https://www.sj... tor/ ⬈	261.4
>	☐	contractor accountants manchester	1 → 1	40	31.01	https://www.sj... ter/ ⬈	583
>	☐	self employed limited company tax	1 → 1	70	0.00	https://www.sj... any/ ⬈	0
>	☐	awr meaning	1 → 1	170	0.00	https://www.sj... ide/ ⬈	0
>	☐	contractor take home pay calculator limited company	1 → 1	90	6.70	https://www.sj... tor/ ⬈	283
>	☐	umbrella company	1 → 1	9,900	34.90	https://www.sj... any/ ⬈	162.4K
>	☐	ir35 for public sector	1 → 1	50	0.00	https://www.sj... tor/ ⬈	0
>	☐	using an umbrella company	1 → 1	90	23.66	https://www.sj... any/ ⬈	1K
>	☐	budget contractors	1 → 1	210	0.00	https://www.sj... rts/ ⬈	0
>	☐	contracting through an umbrella company	1 → 1	40	31.61	https://www.sj... any/ ⬈	593.8
>	☐	agency nurse limited company	1 → 1	70	3.80	https://www.sj... rse/ ⬈	124.5
>	☐	can you be self employed and have a limited company	1 → 1	50	0.00	https://www.sj... any/ ⬈	0
>	☐	contractor pension corporation tax	1 → 1	70	0.00	https://www.sj... ons/ ⬈	0
>	☐	take home pay calculator independent contractor	1 → 1	70	2.91	https://www.sj... tor/ ⬈	95.1
>	☐	nurses setting up a ltd company	1 → 1	70	0.00	https://www.sj... rse/ ⬈	0
>	☐	best umbrella company	1 → 1	720	31.70	https://www.sj... ips/ ⬈	10.7K
>	☐	ebt insurance	1 → 1	50	0.00	https://www.sj... ide/ ⬈	0
>	☐	life as a contractor	1 → 1	50	0.00	https://www.sj... ife/ ⬈	0

To explain the table briefly, the 'Keyword' column shows the phrase they're ranking for. The 'Pos' column shows the position on Google (1 is top of Google. 11 is position 11, which is first on page 2, and so on). 'Volume' is an estimate of the number of times each month that the phrase is searched and 'CPC' is an estimate of how much competitors are spending per click to advertise for that phrase.

The first thing to notice from the chart is that their article about umbrella companies has got them ranking in top position for "umbrella company". The cost of advertising for this keyword would be in the region of £35 per click, so this page alone is bringing them an estimated £162,000 worth of traffic *per month* for that keyword. However, there are a ton of other related keywords that this page is also ranking for, so the actual value is likely significantly higher.

The SJD site also has a contractor take home pay calculator, which is a massive source of traffic for them. They're ranking in position 3 for "contractor salary calculator", so certainly could be doing better, but with this calculator ranking on page 1 for a combined 15,000 searches per month, it's likely to be a very profitable source of leads.

So why did they build a take home pay calculator for contractors? They sell their accountancy services to contractors, who would be searching for this term and would find the calculator useful. Here's the calculator page:

Our contractor take home pay calculator is designed to assess your earning potential.

Our take home pay calculator uses your hourly or daily rate, amongst other factors, to evaluate your potential monthly income after deductions. Calculations are based on the below assumptions:

1) 18/19 tax and NIC rate
2) Flat Rate Scheme for VAT with first year discount applied
3) Business expenses are estimated at 5% of net annual invoice total
4) Income taken out of the company is only up to basic rate thresholds
5) You are a limited cost trader
6) You are eligible for entrepreneur's relief
7) You work 52 weeks per full tax year

From our 28 years' experience, we know take home pay is a determining factor when deciding to become an independent professional. Our salary calculator has been designed to help you realise your earning potential.

Note that these calculations are only an estimate and are only applicable to assignments outside IR35.

To get started, simply enter your hourly or daily rate.

VIEW GUIDES

If you're interested in an example of how take home pay as a contractor differs between limited companies and umbrella companies, this comparison gives a good overview. You can also find out more about how National Insurance Contributions and the Flat Rate VAT Scheme affect your earnings in this article.

Besides these aspects, it is likely that you will have other questions when it comes to starting your contracting career; for example expenses, the flat rate VAT scheme and IR35 are things that you may like to know about. At SJD Accountancy we have over 28 years of contractor accounting experience, so you can be assured that when you appoint us to be your accountant, you're in good hands.

Need a little help to decide?

The simplest way is to call us on 01442 353 465, we'll have a friendly dedicated member of our team waiting to go through your unique contracting needs and recommend the package that's right for you. Or, you can request a callback at a time to suit you, with the form below

We want you to know exactly how our service works and why we need your details. Please read our Privacy Policy before you continue.

118

Notice how the page starts off informative, giving the visitor exactly what they came for. It then moves into offering their accountancy services to the page visitor, which is how they get clients.

They use the information to bring people in then have a clear call-to-action to turn the visitors into buyers. It's so simple and so effective.

The second thing I want to point out about this site is how important, or unimportant, the homepage is to their rankings:

URL	Traffic	Traffic %	Keywords	Ads keywords	Backlinks
https://www.sjdaccountancy.com/resources/umbrella-company/using-an-umbrella-company/	4.9K	28.71	72	0	Show
https://www.sjdaccountancy.com/ ← Homepage	3.2K	18.88	354	0	Show
https://www.sjdaccountancy.com/contractor-calculator/	1.7K	10.02	1K	0	Show
https://www.sjdaccountancy.com/resources/limited-company/ebt-employe...it-trust-guide/	1.2K	6.87	20	0	Show
https://www.sjdaccountancy.com/our-services/sjd-online/	1.1K	6.58	52	0	Show
https://www.sjdaccountancy.com/resources/umbrella-company/choosing-u...a-company-tips/	379	2.20	10	0	Show
https://www.sjdaccountancy.com/resources/ir35/inside-ir35/	225	1.30	51	0	Show
https://www.sjdaccountancy.com/resources/ir35/calculator/	199	1.15	10	0	Show
https://www.sjdaccountancy.com/resources/financial-advice/flat-rate-vat-scheme-guide/	198	1.15	404	0	Show
https://www.sjdaccountancy.com/resources/limited-company/advantages-disadvantages/	187	1.08	152	0	Show
https://www.sjdaccountancy.com/resources/becoming-contractor/sole-tra...imited-company/	169	0.98	97	0	Show
https://www.sjdaccountancy.com/resources/becoming-contractor/choosing-accountant/	166	0.96	14	0	Show
https://www.sjdaccountancy.com/resources/ir35/public-sector/	155	0.90	59	0	Show
https://www.sjdaccountancy.com/resources/financial-advice/contractor-pensions/	148	0.86	329	0	Show
https://www.sjdaccountancy.com/resources/umbrella-company/awr-guide/	134	0.77	29	0	Show
https://www.sjdaccountancy.com/resources/limited-company/self-employed-limited-company/	112	0.65	176	0	Show
https://www.sjdaccountancy.com/resources/umbrella/choosing-umbrella-company-tips/	109	0.63	17	0	Show
https://www.sjdaccountancy.com/resources/becoming-contractor/ltd-vs-umbrella/	108	0.62	84	0	Show
https://www.sjdaccountancy.com/resources/limited-company/tax-benefits-...ployed-limited/	101	0.58	250	0	Show
https://www.sjdaccountancy.com/resources/financial-advice/budget-reports/	101	0.58	6	0	Show
https://www.sjdaccountancy.com/resources/limited-company/psc-guide/	91	0.52	12	0	Show
https://www.sjdaccountancy.com/new-contractor/	78	0.45	18	0	Show
https://www.sjdaccountancy.com/resources/ir35/ir35-rules/	77	0.44	20	0	Show
https://www.sjdaccountancy.com/resources/limited-company/how-take-mo...imited-company/	77	0.44	201	0	Show
https://www.sjdaccountancy.com/resources/becoming-contractor/how-to-contract/	73	0.42	20	0	Show
https://www.sjdaccountancy.com/resources/sector-advice/limited-company-agency-nurse/	72	0.41	79	0	Show
https://www.sjdaccountancy.com/contact/midlands/birmingham/	72	0.41	5		

Most underperforming websites find that their homepage is the page which ranks for the most keywords. They rely on this page to do most of the legwork because their subpages are poorly optimised or aren't clear about the keywords that they're targeting. The SJD homepage contributes a mere 18.88% of their rankings.

If you took away this Knowledge Base section from the SJD Accountancy website, you'd be depriving the website of the vast majority of its ranking and traffic. In fact, they'd lose about 80% of their traffic.

In other words, that knowledge base and the information pages on the site have increased the traffic 4X compared to if they weren't following this strategy. For many businesses, that could be the difference between them hitting their growth goals or staying in the frustrating 'struggle zone'.

Okay, so we know that Knowledge Bases and FAQ sections are important. How do you go about creating one for your business?

The full process could well be a book in its own right but I'm going to run you through a brief exercise here that you can do to begin planning and building your Knowledge Base.

More advanced guides and video tutorials are available inside our digital marketing training platform MarketingU, which can be found at www.marketingu.ninja.

Of course, if you'd like some help with your Knowledge Base then get in touch or request a free marketing review at https://exposureninja.com/google-book.

How to Plan a Knowledge Base

The first thing you need to do is identify the content topics that you'll be building your Knowledge Base around. How big you decide to build your Knowledge Base depends on your time or budget but even if you begin with a 5-10 page Knowledge Base focusing on one area of expertise, that's a good start.

You'll want to begin with keyword research. You can use the keyword research process from Section 1 of this book to draw up a long-list of informational keyword searches to target.

Let's do an example for an eCommerce store selling bathroom furniture (baths, showers, sinks, toilets etc). It doesn't matter whether or not you're an eCommerce site or whether or not you sell bathrooms, this same *process* will work for you.

I want to get this Ninja Bathrooms site ranking but I'm facing some stiff competition, so I'll need to be smart about how I start chipping away at this market. A Knowledge Base could be perfect here because this is likely to be a topic that people are searching for advice and help with and those people could be great potential customers.

From my keyword research, I've established that there is a good search volume for phrases around "bathroom styles". I've identified particular styles that would be great for me to target, as I have an excellent selection of products in those styles. I decide that my target phrases for my Knowledge Base are going to be around:

Content Category	Target Keyword	Search Volume for Keyword
Styles	Bathroom styles	320
	Bathroom style ideas	110
Victorian	Victorian style bathrooms	320
	Victorian style bathroom tiles	140
	Victorian style bathroom suites	140
	Victorian style bathroom accessories	50
Country	Country style bathrooms	170
	Country style bathroom sinks	90
	Country style bathroom ideas	90

Notice that I've categorised my target keywords into logical groups; a general, introductory 'Styles' section and more specific 'Victorian' and 'Country' sections.

By the way, I've put together a spreadsheet you can use during this process. To download it, visit https://exposureninja.com/google-book-freebies.

From here, I can begin to see the sort of shape my Knowledge Base will take. I'm also going to call my Knowledge Base, "Bathroom Style Guide", because that's more descriptive than the phrase "Knowledge Base". Remember that at this stage, I'm starting fairly small. You will want to add to your Knowledge Base over time and it doesn't have to be 'finished' in order to go live.

Using the bullet point annotation we described earlier, we can start to plan out a rough structure:

- Bathroom Style Guide (this will be an overview page, summarising the different styles in my Knowledge Base).
  - o Bathroom style ideas (some pictures and descriptions of different styles)
  - o How to choose a bathroom style (tips on how to work sympathetically to the property etc.)
  - o Victorian Style Bathrooms (overview page packed full of information about this style e.g. the different pieces in a Victorian style bathroom, each with links to the pages below with even more detail. This page will also target "Victorian style bathroom ideas" phrases)
    - ▪ Victorian bathroom sinks (in-depth guide to Victorian bathroom sinks)

- Victorian baths (in-depth guide to Victorian baths)
- Victorian bathroom tiles (in-depth guide to Victorian bathroom tiles)
- Victorian bathroom accessories(in-depth guide to Victorian bathroom accessories)
  - o Country Style Bathrooms (again, an overview page targeting "ideas" phrases)
    - Country style bathroom sinks
    - Country style baths
    - etc.

From this simple exercise, you can see how simple it would be to build up a formidable Knowledge Base of in-depth content around these topics.

Even if you have eCommerce category pages targeting some of these phrases, it's likely that these Knowledge Base pages will outrank them on your site because they are so informative. Of course, you'll want to make sure that your Knowledge Base pages link to your relevant products and category pages throughout because traffic without conversion is simply charity.

By taking this approach and slowly working through your product or service categories, you can start to build the sort of content base worthy of making your site dominant in its market.

CHAPTER 15

How to use your Blog to Actually Make Money

"I've tried blogging. I wrote quite a lot of posts with updates about our business, new products, events and anything else newsworthy. The posts just don't get any readers and they *definitely* don't lead to new business." **Sound familiar?**

If it does, I want to suggest a completely different approach to your blog. In fact, it's an approach that can turn your blog from being a waste of time and server space to one of your greatest digital marketing assets. Best of all, it works in *any* market. Sold?

At the time of writing this, our blog brings in around 79% of all our website traffic each week. This proportion is not uncommon amongst clients for whom we've been working on blogs for more than a year.

What's more, the vast majority of this traffic is completely *cold*, meaning it's new potential customers who never would have heard of Exposure Ninja otherwise (until they bought this book).

Here's how this blogging strategy works. Rather than treating your blog as a 'newsfeed' (read: a place to dump boring 'news' that literally no-one outside the company cares about), treat it as a place to answer audience questions and give them useful information that they genuinely care about.

When people search for these questions on Google, your extremely well-written, in-depth and super useful blog post is going to show up for that question. They're going to click on your post, read your recommendations and insight and, if they like what they see and you offer them a clear and compelling next step, they might sign up or become a lead.

Think that seems too good to be true? If you choose the right questions and write a genuinely *awesome* post, it's actually pretty easy to get these blog posts ranking well.

If this all feels a bit theoretical, the graph below shows a client that we used this strategy on:

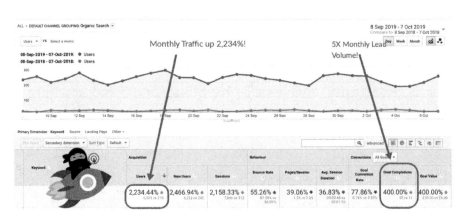

This graph compares the same period year on year. We managed to increase this website's traffic from search from a measly 270 visitors per month to 6,303 per month. Lead volume increased from 11 leads to 55 leads in the same timeframe.

The main ingredient of this success? The blog posts we wrote for them.

The client is a solicitors firm specialising in a particular type of divorce law. We researched and wrote a series of posts on the topic that picked up really strong rankings for the questions potential clients had about this topic. Their blog posts have gone from being dull and boring 'news' about the inner workings of the firm (yawn) to interesting information, precisely targeted and highly visible to the sort of potential clients they want to attract.

So, want to know which questions to write about for your business? Here's how we'd approach this for clients and for ourselves:

Step 1: Brainstorm topics. Start off by thinking about what your area of expertise is. We're going to use an example of a company that arranges corporate events. Their area of expertise is fabulous, unique and exciting events which their clients can bring customers, staff and contacts to. Their expert knowledge is in areas such as catering, venues and entertainment. You can also check https://buzzsumo.com to see what sort of content tends to get the most shares in each topic area.

Step 2: Find the questions people are asking. Next, go to https://answerthepublic.com. Type in your specialist area ("corporate events") and hit enter, and it'll show you the most common questions that people ask about this topic, taken from the question suggestions on Google. Taking our corporate events example, we get questions like:

- How to plan corporate events
- How to book corporate events
- How to market corporate events
- Why corporate events are important
- What is a corporate event planner
- What is corporate event management
- Are corporate events tax deductible
- <u>What are corporate events</u>
- <u>What does corporate events mean</u>

Some of these questions could be asked by potential clients of a corporate events planner and some asked by people who definitely *aren't* because they're so basic. I've underlined these ones. There are also some in the middle, which I've left in for now.

So, we now have some questions that people are likely to ask. I'm going to add a few more off the top of my head which I think could be interesting:

- How far in advance should you organise corporate events
- Why use a corporate events planner
- How big does a corporate event need to be
- What are common corporate event mistakes
- How do you come up with corporate event ideas

AlsoAsked (https://alsoasked.com) is another great tool for researching which types of questions people are searching for. It looks at the "People Also Asked" box you see on search result pages and pulls out all the possible questions.

Step 3: Check search volumes. You don't want to slave over an incredible blog post only to find that you've written about something no-one is searching for. Head over to Semrush (try it for free at https://thankyouninjas.com) and start testing out your questions to see what the search volumes look like.

A quick tip though, Google's approach to keywords is far more sophisticated than any of these tools, so you want to take all keyword volumes with a fairly hefty pinch of salt. Your blog post can (and will, if it's decent) show up for lots of related questions and variants, which the tools won't reflect in their search volumes. Also, think about the *quality* of the searchers. Some-one searching for "how to plan a corporate event" could be a pretty tasty lead, so even if there are only fifty of them per month, we'll take them.

My advice with keyword research here is like my advice with keyword research for your main site; don't let the data overrule your gut feeling and knowledge of your business. I've said it a million times; that very first website I made for my next door neighbour *changed his life*, ranking top for a keyword that all the tools said there was *no* search volume for.

Step 4: Plan your post. Just like writing a book, it's a good idea to start with headings. You'll want to make the blog post title the main phrase that you're targeting and your headings will usually be clarification questions.

Looking at our example corporate events website, the first blog post I've decided to write is "How to plan corporate events: the complete beginners guide".

I've used my target keyword at the start and called out my target audience by adding "the complete beginners guide". To plan the sections in my post, I'm going to think of the most important subtopics:

- How to choose a corporate events theme
- Finding the perfect venue
- How to plan the catering
- Finding great corporate events entertainment
- Using an events planner vs managing DIY

You might be thinking that each of these subheadings could make great individual posts, and you're right! Once this post is published, we can then add more detailed posts covering the separate topics and link to these from the initial post. That'll give those shorter, but more specific posts an even better chance of ranking for their target phrases.

Step 5: Write your post. When it comes to writing your blog post, make it really detailed, fantastically useful and show off your best knowledge. Imagine that you're going to be on stage in front of a room full of potential customers reading this post out to them, you'd want to make it your best work, right? I'm not going to give you a target word count because high-ranking blog posts can be anything from 300 words to 10,000 words. Just remember, Google wants to show the very *best* content prominently in its results. So if you can demonstrate that this blog post is better than any other on the topic, you earn the right to rank prominently.

Your blog is going to need a compelling title, which means that people should want to click on it and be able to tell what it's about from the description. We're not going for Buzzfeed-style clickbait here though e.g. "5 Corporate Event Themes You'll Wish You Could Unsee". Remember that the point of the exercise is to use a title which closely matches what your audience searches for so that it ranks well on Google.

Step 6: Optimise and publish. Before you publish your post, it's worth running through some optimisation to make sure it has the best chance of ranking once it's live.

Here are some of the checks we do when we're writing client blog posts—it's a tried and tested formula!

- Does this blog use only one H1 heading? Remember that this is the heading type to give your main blog title.
- Are the other post headings properly assigned H2, H3 tags etc?
- Are there clear calls to action (CTAs) at the end of the post and throughout so readers know what they need to do next if they want to buy from you?
- Does the blog link out to other websites where necessary? Although it's best not to link to competitors or low-quality websites.

- Do these links open in a new tab? You don't want visitors closing your site when they click on your blog links.

- Does the blog use internal links to point readers to your product or service pages?

- Is relevant anchor text used on all links?

- Is your main target keyword or key phrase found a) in the title, b) in at least one heading and c) in the first 100 words of the text?

- Does the post use related keywords as well?

- Does your blog post include interesting images? Pure text blogs can be pretty boring to read. These images should have titles and alt tags (see the 'Image Optimisation' section)

- Is the spelling and grammar mistake free, as checked by Grammarly (www.grammarly.com)?

- Is the blog clear and easy to read, as checked by the Hemingway app (https://hemingwayapp.com)?

- Have you added optimised page titles and meta descriptions (see the 'Behind the scenes optimisation' section next)?

Further Resources

We've written some detailed guides on how to write Ninja blog posts for your website so if you'd like to truly master writing great (and profitable) blogs, sign up for lifetime updates of this book at https://exposureninja.com/google-book and we'll email you these guides as well.

Hopefully you can now see a path to writing blogs that have a genuine and measurable business impact, not just in 'awareness', but in things that are measurable e.g. traffic, leads and sales.

CHAPTER 16

Behind the scenes Optimisation

As well as optimising what you *can* see on your website for Google, there are a few crucial yet simple things you can do *behind the scenes* to push its ranking up.

The Fastest Way to Improve your Ranking: Writing Killer Page Titles

Word for word, page titles are *the most important* SEO element of your entire site. They indicate to Google and visitors which phrases you think each page should rank for. This title shows up in the visitor's browser tab and is shown by Google in the search results as the headline for each page. For these reasons, it's obviously important that your page titles are descriptive, appealing and include your target keywords.

Every page on your website should have a page title. This is a bit of behind the scenes code which may or may not be the same as your page's headline (the *visible* text at the top of the page). Usually, your page title and page headline should *not* be the same and here we'll explore why. Before we do, here's how to set your page title in WordPress:

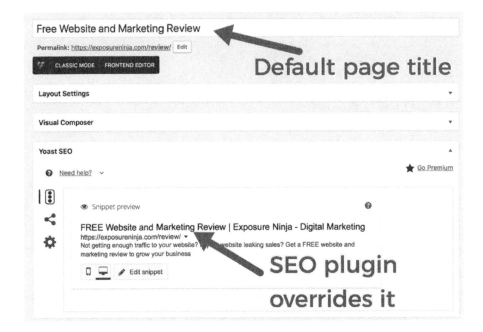

In this example, we have the Yoast SEO plugin installed. The settings in Yoast will automatically override the default Word-Press page title. This is a good thing, because it means that you can set the default title to something that has meaning for you and you can set the public-facing page title to something that is optimised for search and visitors.

In Google search results, a page title longer than about 60 characters will be truncated. So, if possible, try to keep under this in order to control exactly what is shown to searchers (we aim to keep titles under 55 characters).

To explain what makes a good page title, let's use an example of a site that was sent to us to review, which sells beautiful custom fitted kitchens in Exmouth, UK. Their current homepage title is set as:

Your Kitchen

```
<title>Your Kitchen</title>
```

That means this is what shows up in search results as:

And in browser tabs:

Whilst this is their brand name, this is a terrible waste of a page title because it says nothing about the business and includes none of their target keywords. A much stronger page title would be:

Custom Fitted Kitchens in Exmouth | Your Kitchen

In this title, we have their main target phrase, location and brand. This template can be used across the site and tweaked to be made relevant for each page. For example, the page targeting natural wood kitchens can use the title:

Fitted Wood Kitchens in Exmouth | Your Kitchen

Searchers that have typed "Wood Kitchens Exmouth" into Google are going to be particularly tuned to that phrase so when they see the top result using those three words, that's going to lead to a higher click-through rate (CTR), solidifying ranking and bringing the business more traffic.

The best ranking page titles usually use the page's target keywords at the start, a variation or two (if there is space), location (if relevant) and the business's brand name at the end. My advice is to go and have a look at the page titles that your top ranking competitors are using.

How you set your page titles will depend on your website platform. You've seen how it's set in WordPress but Shopify, BigCommerce, Squarespace and other platforms all have their own settings. Magento users, for example, can install an 'SEO Titles' plugin, which will allow them to change their page titles without affecting the name of the page in menus or throughout the Magento backend.

Meta Descriptions

You'll remember the <meta name="description"... from our competitor analysis section. You might also remember that this is the descriptive text that usually shows up in the Google results so this is our chance to pitch potential website visitors on why they should click on our site rather than the competition.

Google announced in 2009 that meta descriptions did *not* contribute to rankings so there's no need to stuff them full of your keywords. However, if your meta descriptions can encourage more people to click on your site than other sites on the search results page, this will be a positive signal to Google that your website is relevant ("Wow, look at all these people clicking on this website in position 7! Perhaps it deserves better ranking!"). For that reason, it's a good idea to make your meta description as enticing as possible. Even though Google doesn't analyse keywords used in meta descriptions, you'll still want to include your target keywords because these are likely to have been the terms that the searcher used to find your site in the first place.

You usually set your meta descriptions around the same place as you set your page titles. They are sometimes labelled "SEO description" or "page description":

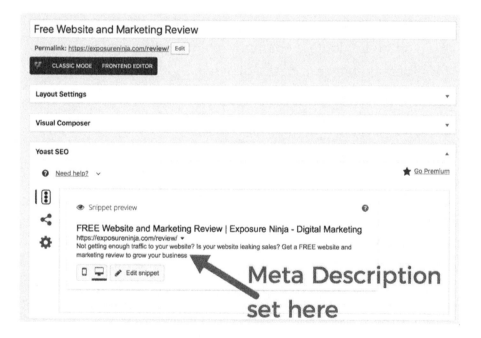

As with any of this stuff, if you are unsure how to change your meta descriptions in your particular website platform, a quick Google search should give you the guidance you need.

One final thing to note before we go into meta descriptions in further detail is that if you *don't* specify meta descriptions, Google will simply pull text copy from your page that it deems relevant. Sometimes this works out, sometimes it really doesn't (as we'll see in a minute). Either way, you will hopefully be better at writing a short advert for your website than Google would, so it's a good idea to write your own.

Once you know *how* to change your meta description, what should you write? Here are my top tips for writing killer meta descriptions:

1. You want it to be enticing to your potential customers. Using boring generic text is never a good idea, so lazy and meaningless company slogans about 'best prices, best quality' are best... avoided. Stating your main USP or a specific compelling feature that sets you apart from your competition can work well, for example, "free 24-hour delivery".

2. Use your keywords by all means but you really don't need to *stuff* your meta description full of them, as it won't help ranking and it'll make your site look like junk in the search results. It's definitely worth including keywords to demonstrate relevance and match what your searcher is looking for, but be selective about it.

3. Google will only show up to a range of 155-160 characters so we recommend playing it safe around the 150-155 character mark. It's not the end of the world if your meta description is shorter than that but the more space you have to play with, the more you can sell the

click to the visitor and the more space your website will take up in search results.

4. If you sell directly from your website, it's a good idea to make this obvious in your meta descriptions. Using phrases like "free delivery available" or "next day delivery on all orders" not only gives you the edge on competitors who *don't* offer such services but also immediately communicates that this is an eCommerce website.

5. If you offer a free consultation, assessment, marketing review, or some other initial free widget to entice people to start doing business with you, mention this in your meta descriptions. Like mentioning free or fast delivery, this will attract high 'commercial intent' searchers (those who are most ready to buy now) and searchers who are action-oriented. These folk are usually easiest to convert into leads and sales so they're certainly the sort of peeps we want on the site!

Let's look at some examples of good and bad meta descriptions now. We'll also see examples of meta descriptions that have been written versus those that have been automatically generated by Google from text on the page.

Land Rover Nottingham - Stratstone
www.stratstone.com/dealers/land-rover-nottingham/ ▾
The team at **Land Rover Nottingham** are one of the most established **Land Rover dealerships** in the country with a standout team which has been recognised for innovation in the workplace for the last 3 years running. Staff at **Land Rover Nottingham** have shown what great teamwork and great customer service can produce ...

In this first example, no meta description has been manually added so Google has used the first paragraph of copy from the page instead. Good or bad? The thing that comes across in this example is that there's absolutely no focus on the customer, products or services, it's 100% about the people that work there. As a customer of this business, I don't care if your dealer is established. I don't care if you're 'innovative' (what does that mean anyway?). All I care about is; will you service my Range Rover Sport? From this meta description, I have no idea.

www.theaa.com › used-cars › used-ford ▾
Used Ford Cars for Sale, Second Hand & Nearly New Ford ...
Used Ford from AA Cars with free breakdown cover. Find the right **used Ford** for you today from AA trusted dealers across the UK.

This meta description has been written manually and, as a result, it's a great length. It tells us what the business does, it gives benefits ("free breakdown cover"), gives us location information ("trusted dealers across the UK") and tells us the goal of the page ("Find the right used Ford...").

One final example:

Land Rover North One
www.landrovernorthone.co.uk/ ▾
CONTACT, WELCOME TO **LAND ROVER** NORTH ONE. **Land Rover** North One Unit 5. Bush Industrial Estate Station Road Tufnell Park **London** N19 5UN. Tel: 0207 561 4860. Fax: 0207 272 6953 info@landrovernorthone.co.uk. We would like to welcome you to our friendly, fully authorised service centre **Land Rover** North ...

This is what happens when there's no meta description and Google fails to generate anything useful. The combination of shouty capitals, little actual info and wasted space taken up by contact information means the click-through rate on this would be low. I mean, look, they've even got a fax number in their meta description! A *fax*. Perhaps someone will fax them a copy of this book.

One final thought on meta descriptions before we move on; using testimonials inside your meta descriptions can be very useful, particularly if they are descriptive. It's a great way for you to powerfully emphasise the things that people love about you without having to directly say it. So, if you offer the best products in your market, your service goes way above and beyond, or you're the undisputed master of your universe but too modest to say it, use a testimonial to get the message across instead.

Meta Keywords

Often, if you see a box allowing you to insert a meta description and page title for your webpage, you will also see a box for you to input 'Meta Keywords'. It is a nice idea that we can just type in our target keywords and Google will pop us a bit of extra ranking!

Unfortunately, the internet hasn't been *this* easy for over a decade and Google simply ignores the meta keywords tag because it is so easy to manipulate. In the olden days of the internet, meta keywords held more weight. Nowadays, their biggest function is showing SEOs from your competition which keywords you have considered important and would like to rank for, saving them the time it takes to do the research for themselves.

We don't recommend spending any time adding meta key-words.

Image Optimisation

When you use images on your website, you'll have the option to set 'alt text'. You might have seen alt text on pages where the image hasn't loaded.

The most important use of alt text is by those with sight issues who use text-to-speech software to describe what's on a page. Secondary to that, Google uses it to understand what the image is about (although their image analysis software is impeccable these days).

Google's guidelines state that alt text "provides Google with useful information about the subject matter of the image." So, it's logical that we want to show Google that the images on our pages are relevant to our target keywords by using them in our images.

Let's look at examples directly from Google's own guidelines. We're looking at the text inside the quotation marks after *alt=* bit:

Not so good:
<img src="puppy.jpg" alt=""/>

You can see that the bit inside the alt= quotation marks is empty. This is what happens when no alt tag is set.

Better:

```
<img src="puppy.jpg" alt="puppy"/>
```

The bit inside the quotation marks says "puppy". Aww. It describes approximately what's in the picture, but not exactly.

Best:
```
<img src="puppy.jpg" alt="Dalmatian puppy playing fetch">
```

"Dalmatian puppy playing fetch" is a much clearer description.

You'll also notice that the image file name (puppy.jpg) is also optimised i.e. it's not img_123093.jpg. This means that before the image was uploaded, it was renamed as something (reasonably) descriptive. Same rules apply here; descriptive is *good*, keyword stuffed spam is *bad*.

Schema Markup

Schema is a set of tags that you can add to your website's code to make certain additional things show up in search results. With fewer than a third of websites using it, Schema is a chance for you to immediately pick up an advantage.

For example, notice here how Amazon used to use Schema to mark up the reviews for this book so that when it showed up in search results, the average review stars also showed up:

How To Get to the Top of Google - The Plain English Guide to SEO ...
https://www.amazon.co.uk/How-Get-Top-Google-including-ebook/.../B0076XVNM8 ▾
★★★★⯪ Rating: 4.5 - 185 reviews
"Having read it cover to cover and mind mapped all the nuggets of information I created three new pages. A week down the line I decided to check to see if the site was appearing on Google, not only was it appearing it was on page 1 for all the key phrases we had chosen and for a few we hadn't!!" - S Woolger --Amazon

Unfortunately, Google removed the ability to mark-up review stars as Amazon used to. However, there are still lots of important markup that we use for clients to help their content to rank well or look better (or bigger) in the search results, including:

- Event information
- Contact and location information for local businesses
- TV episode and film details
- Restaurant information
- Product information

In total, there are almost 600 different types of data and it's beyond the scope of this book to go through each one in detail.

If you're on WordPress, there are plenty of plugins (just search "Schema plugin") that can handle the legwork for you without you having to get sticky in code.

Once you've added your Schema, you can test it using Schema.org's Markup Validator (https://validator.schema.org) to ensure that it's being read properly.

I should also note that adding Schema to your website doesn't guarantee that Google will show it in search results. As with pretty much everything in this book, all you can do is give Google what it needs to show the Schema. Ultimately, the decision to show or not show depends on whether the algorithm considers the information to be useful to the searcher or not.

CHAPTER 17

Website Speed Hacks

Your website's speed has a significant effect on its success. Historically, website speed has always been important for ranking at the top of Google. Over the last few years, as Google has put more importance on the mobile web experience, website speed has become one the algorithm's core ranking requirements. We've even seen websites increase their ranking rapidly simply by switching to a faster hosting server.

In June 2021, Google launched the "Page Experience" update which introduced Core Web Vitals as ranking factors (https://developers.google.com/search/blog/2021/04/more-details-page-experience), the biggest speed-focused algorithm update to date.

Core Web Vitals are a complicated way of measuring the speed-based usability of a website. There are multiple scores a website will have to perform well on, some of them have technical names, like Cumulative Layout Shift, which nobody other than website developers understand (it measures how much a web page moves as it continues to load on slower connections).

These important speed assessments can be found within Google's PageSpeed Insights tool, which you can use for free here: https://developers.google.com/speed/pagespeed/insights

It's easy to get wrapped up in the results of these tools, especially when some numbers are bold and red in colour, but they should only be used as a guide. Reaching a perfect score takes a lot of effort and for many businesses it won't be worth the financial investment.

Where website speed is *most* important is on mobile devices. According to Google's Maile Ohye, the impact of a website taking an extra one second to load on a smartphone is a drop in page views of 9.4%. That's nearly 10% fewer pages being viewed on your site for just a one second increase. But it also hurts profit; the same additional second caused a 3.4% reduction in conversions. Internet users are impatient and, on mobile, this impatience gets ramped up significantly.

Human Response Times: The 3 Important Limits

Jakob Neilsen's book *Usability Engineering* defines three time limits to be taken into consideration for all computer applications. Despite the fact that the book was published in 1993, the figures still hold true, as humans have not evolved significantly in 20 years. If anything, our attention spans have actually *shortened* so these numbers could be slightly generous!

- 0.1 second is the threshold for website users to feel that the site or application is responding to them *in real time*.

- 1 second is the limit for the user's thought flow to stay uninterrupted. They'll notice the delay but they'll be in approximately the same place they were when you left them.

- 10 seconds is the limit for keeping their attention. Thoughts will have wandered or they might start doing other things, so for delays as long or longer than 10 seconds, we need to provide visual feedback to let them know when the site will be loaded.

As you can see, one-second page loading is the target to aim for so that we're keeping maximum engagement with the site.

According to a Kissmetrics study, 47% of web users expect a page to load within two seconds and 40% of people abandon a site that takes longer than three seconds to load. They also claim that an additional second of loading hurts conversion rate by 7%. For a business bringing in £1,000 of enquiries per day, this one second will cost £25,000 each year.

Measuring your Website's Performance

When I wrote this book, website speed wasn't spoken about at all. Today, every business owner, marketing manager and website administrator bears the responsibility of making sure their website is quick, even if they're not technically minded, and that's okay. There's a lot you can do with very limited technical skills or resources.

There are a variety of free tools online to help you measure and diagnose any website speed issues you might have. The two we recommend most often are Google's PageSpeed Insights (https://developers.google.com/speed/pagespeed/insights), which highlights any potential issues and suggests solutions, and the Pingdom Website Speed Test (https://tools.pingdom. com), which gives a 'waterfall' breakdown, showing you how long your site takes to load and which elements are responsible for the delays.

While detailed technical instructions for speeding up every part of your website are beyond the scope of this book, here is our list of the most common problem areas:

- **Leverage Browser Caching.** Your website is made up of lots of different files, including images, CSS, HTML and Javascript files. Not all of these files need to be downloaded every time someone returns to your site because many of these files are unlikely to change from one day to the next. So, to save time and bandwidth, browsers cache these files. Through your site's settings, you tell the browsers how often they need to 'refresh' these files and obviously the longer the period between refreshes, the fewer downloads are required so the faster the page will reload. For WordPress users, we recommend installing W3 Total Cache, which handles this automatically.

- **Reduce Server Response Time.** This metric shows how long the server takes to respond to the request for the files. If the server is slow, the site is slow to load. Low-budget hosting can be a cause of long response times, particularly if you're on a shared hosting plan, because you could be lumped in with a huge number of other websites, all fighting for limited resources.

- **Optimise Images.** Image files can usually be compressed without losing quality, which means shorter download times. WordPress users can use EWWW Image Optimizer to automatically optimise the images on their site.

- **Prioritise Visible Content.** If your website loads visible content first, this will give the illusion that the site has loaded quickly. By prioritising content that appears 'above the fold', you're giving your visitors a better experience and keeping them engaged. Again, the solution to this is quite technical, so it's best to ask your super-geek developer friend for a favour here.

Another website speed factor is server location. If your website's visitors are halfway across the world from your servers, any requests and transfers have to travel halfway across the world to the server and then all the way back to the user! Even when you're moving at the speed of light, all this travel adds delay. By using servers located closer to your audience, you can minimise this delay.

A neat service that helps in this area is Cloudflare (www.cloudflare.com). Cloudflare seeks to help optimise website speed in a number of ways, including through its optimiser and CDN (Content Delivery Network), which stores caches of your sites in each of its data centres around the world. When someone visits your site, the files are sent from the closest data centre, saving them from having to travel across the world. Cloudflare is free for basic accounts and relatively easy to set up, so it's definitely worth a look.

Increasing website speed is too important to ignore but, for most business owners, addressing these sorts of issues *themselves* is an ineffective and unprofitable use of time. It's best to employ someone (or an agency) to do this for you. Our website development team do this all the time, so do send us a message at https://exposureninja.com/contact

CHAPTER 18

Google Search Console

Google Search Console (previously called Webmaster Tools) is a really useful place to monitor how your website is performing in searches. For example, you can see:

- How many times your website appears in Google searches
- How many times searchers clicked on your website
- How many times individual pages showed up in searches
- Your average position in search results
- Which websites are linking to you and how many times
- If your website is suffering from any manual spam penalties
- If Google has identified any security issues with your website

The first thing to do is sign up and add your site to Search Console. Go to https://search.google.com/search-console/ about and follow the instructions to get your account set up if you don't already have one. You'll need to add your website, so click the 'Add property' button and follow the instructions to verify ownership.

Once you've added your website, the first thing you'll want to do is submit your sitemap. This is important because it's likely that your XML sitemap isn't linked to from anywhere on your website, other than your robots.txt file. Without manually submitting it to Google, the Googlebot will have no idea where to look for it.

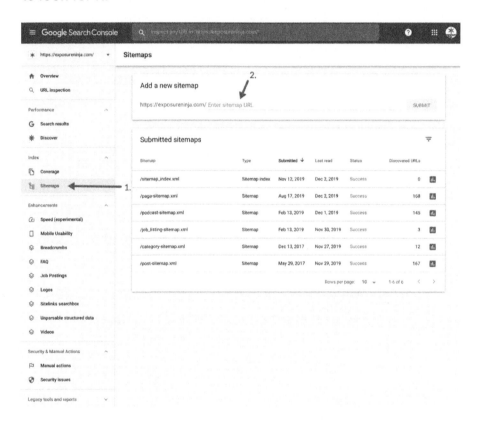

You should see the 'sitemaps' menu option on the left hand side of the screen which will give you a field where you can paste the URL of your sitemap. You'll get a notification that the sitemap has been submitted and that Google will periodically check your sitemap to look for website changes.

Another really useful element inside Search Console is the Search Results section:

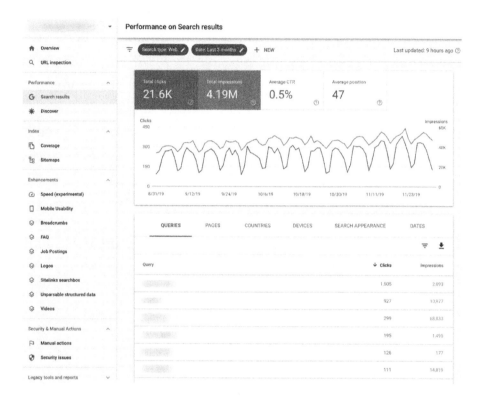

This section shows you the queries (keywords) that your website has shown up for, the number of times it has shown up (impressions) and the number of clicks it has received from Google. This is really useful 'first party' data from Google and is a great way to track your SEO progress over time. You can see in the graph above that both impressions and clicks are increasing over the three month period shown. This is consistent with a website that is working through the principles in this book!

Manual Actions and Reconsideration Requests

One vital section in Search Console is the 'Manual Actions' tab. We often get asked how it's possible to tell if your website is suffering from a 'Google Penalty'. The only type of penalty that results in a notification is a manual penalty applied by Google's webspam team. These penalties are fairly rare and are usually only levied at sites that have been found to violate Google's quality guidelines by being super naughty.

Most of the time, if you go to Fiverr.com* and buy 10,000 backlinks for $5, Google's algorithms will pick up these junk links and simply ignore them. If, however, they slip through the net and someone in the webspam team spots them, your site could be subjected to a manual action.

Fiverr asked me specifically not to refer to them as a source of low quality links. Sorry, Fiverr!

A manual action is basically a manual 'flag' against your site which can reduce or even eliminate its visibility in Google altogether. The most common manual actions are:

- Unnatural links to your website. If you're suffering from this manual penalty, Search Console will list some of the links and you will then need to go and contact the website owners to get them removed.

- A hacked site. If your website has been hacked, it could well be producing spam. Don't worry, it happens to almost everyone at some point. Usually, updating your plugins and refreshing your site's core files will do the trick. In some cases where the hack is deeper, you might need some help. If in doubt, contact Exposure Ninja, as we have a Hacking Ninja on the team who can get you sorted.

If you get a manual action against your website, you should do everything in your power to get the problem solved. Once you do, you'll be able to request a review of your site from the manual action report. Provided you have removed the issue, you should get the manual action lifted.

Note: If you have experienced a manual action penalty and are not sure where to start with recovering your website's ranking, please request your free website review and specify the penalty to our team https://exposureninja.com/review

By now, if you've been following the instructions so far, you should have a well-optimised site which has already seen some impressive ranking improvements. In the next section, we're going to take these improvements to the next level with *offsite promotion*.

SECTION 3

Promoting Your Website

Once you have your website optimised and it is more Google-friendly than an overseas tax haven, it's time to get promoting it online. Promotion is an incredibly important part of getting your website to the top of Google because websites that have lots of quality links pointing at them are much easier to rank. Websites with few or no links pointing at them are unlikely to rank as well, even if they have fantastic content.

In 2016, Andrey Lipattsev, a Google search engineer, confirmed that the three most important elements in SEO are content, links and RankBrain (although that may have changed after Google integrated BERT and MUM into the algorithm).

No area of SEO has changed so dramatically as how links are treated. In the 'olden days' of SEO (usually pre-2011), getting links was as simple as clicking 'buy now' on a website offering links for sale. Link volumes were spoken about in dozens, hundreds, thousands or even tens of thousands, as in, 'buy 10,000 backlinks'. These links were total trash; automated blog comments, 'spun' articles or listings on 'link directories' purely built for SEO. There was only really one rule; *links help ranking*.

Fast forward to today and we live in a much more complex world. Acquiring links today takes a mammoth amount of time and energy because it requires real people to do *real work*. The old automated methods no longer do anything (probably more harm than good), and the new methods have super-strict guidelines. That's why the top SEO companies today either weren't around in the 'olden days' or have changed beyond recognition.

Whilst many lament the 'good old days', for you and I, these changes are fantastic news because they mean that *real* businesses which get *real* attention are the ones that win. Just as 'building a great website' and 'good onsite SEO' are increasingly becoming the same thing, so too is 'doing great online marketing' and 'good offsite SEO'. Google rewards websites that are talked about, covered and mentioned, and it rewards them according to who is doing the talking, covering and mentioning.

So many of the techniques that you'll see in this section are 'just good online marketing'. That's not to say that *all* marketing will help SEO and that ranking increases will just happen automatically. As we'll see throughout, each of these strategies will require a clear SEO focus if we're to extract maximum ranking benefit. However, nothing that we do in this section will have the *sole* benefit of improving ranking. Everything will either raise your profile in your market or give you wider national or international visibility.

This section contains a few things which are going to sound suspiciously like hard work. Celebrate these because lazy competitors won't bother with them. That's how you know which competitors you are most likely to crush first.

CHAPTER 19

Link Acquisition Basics

As we saw in Section 1, Google's PageRank algorithm assigns each page a score based on the links directed to that page. The value of each link depends on the score of the page that the link comes from. This gives Google a simple way to judge the authority of a page and to decide which page a user is most likely to want to see in search results.

Almost all of the SEO world uses a metric called Domain Authority to measure the importance of a link. Domain Authority, or DA, is a metric established and calculated by Moz and is supposed to approximate the authority of a website in Google's eyes. The original idea was that it was designed to run using a basic version of Google's PageRank algorithm. A website like the BBC, for example, has a Domain Authority of 100/100, meaning it's considered one of the most authoritative websites around and is more likely to rank for the phrases it targets than a website with a lower DA. We'll revisit DA shortly.

If you've been in business even for a little while, you'll almost certainly have links to your website already. Some of these might be from suppliers, niche websites in your market, directories, or your social pages. You might have had some press attention too and, if you've done any previous SEO work, then obviously those links will be there as well.

CHAPTER 20

Good links vs Bad links

We're often asked by confused business owners, "how do I know which links are *good* ones worth working for and which are the *bad* ones that can get me penalised?" I'll give you the simple answer and then we'll dig around in more detail.

The simple answer is that any time you get a link from a website that people *actually visit* and enjoy going to, it's usually a good link:

- Links from established and popular websites are usually the most authoritative and powerful.
- Links from websites that exist purely for SEO purposes (with names like linkdirectory123.biz) are usually trash and won't do you any favours.
- Links from websites that are authorities *on your topic* are considered to be high-quality, as topical relevance is important.
- A brand new website might have low authority metrics but if the website is legit and useful, then a link from the website would be good to have.

Are you suffering from a Link Penalty?

A lot of the fear these days about bad links is misplaced. In 2012, when Google released its Penguin update, we saw a lot of sites dropped from search results completely, purely because they had been using junk SEO companies that got them tons of low-quality links. It happened literally overnight; site owners woke to find their traffic had dropped off a cliff and, within days, businesses were struggling as a result.

To regain this ranking, we had to try to remove the links, 'disavow' the rest and rebuild the site's authority in a legitimate way. During this period, we managed to save all but one of the websites that were sent our way. Nevertheless, the fear that this period struck into the hearts of website owners around the world remains.

With Google's final Penguin update in September 2016 (before it made Penguin "real-time" and constantly running in the broader algorithm), it announced that bad links would no longer bring a 'penalty', as such, but would instead simply be *ignored*. Since this update, low-quality links should not have the extreme negative impact that they did between 2012 and 2016.

In my experience, most website owners who believe that their sites are being penalised are mistaken. They see that they had strong rankings and that these have been declining, so assume that Google is slowly punishing them. What's usually happening, however, is one of three things:

1. They used to rely on lots of junk links for their rankings at a time when junk links helped. These junk links are

now ignored and the benefit is gone. This can *look* like a penalty, when it's really just a correction.

2. They have not continued to work on updating and promoting their website and, as a result, competitors are slowly overtaking them. This usually appears as a gradual decline over many months.

3. They have an issue (e.g., their website is not mobile-friendly, it loads really slowly, there's hardly any text, etc.), which Google's algorithms are picking up on and giving more priority than they were previously. This can show as a fairly steep drop following an algorithm update, which is why it can look like a penalty.

In all cases like these, the solution is to follow the steps in this book to run proper SEO, make a good website, promote it. This work is not something that is ever 'finished', unfortunately, and treating it as such is likely to result in a gradual decline in rankings.

Link Metrics

If you want to get a bit more scientific about your link analysis, or you have a large number of links that you want to analyse and you don't have time to visit every single website, there are some useful metrics you can use.

It's important to note that these metrics are neither 'official Google metrics', nor are they strictly necessary. In fact, it's possible to run an excellent SEO campaign without giving any regard to these metrics. As these metrics are maintained by third-party companies, they also tend to be created by far cruder algorithms than the ones Google is likely to be using. In addition, because they're not official Google algorithms, they're likely to give different results to Google's own.

In my seminars, I often warn the audience about relying on data which appears to be exact but is built on rather basic assumptions or even complete guesswork. So, whilst these metrics are useful and can be a shortcut to carrying out an impossible amount of research on every website, we must always remember to take them with a pinch of salt. Whenever you have to decide between trusting data and common sense, in SEO, you'll usually want to follow the latter.

With that said, here is a guide to some of the most popular link metrics:

Domain Authority (DA)

We touched on DA briefly earlier on. From Moz.com: Domain Authority (DA) is a search engine ranking score developed by Moz that predicts how well a website will rank on search engine result pages (SERPs). A Domain Authority score ranges from one to 100, with higher scores corresponding to a greater ability to rank.

Domain Authority is calculated by evaluating linking root domains, number of total links, MozRank (https://moz.com/learn/seo/mozrank), MozTrust (https://moz.com/learn/seo/moztrust) and similar statistics into a single DA score. This score can then be used when comparing websites or tracking the "ranking strength" of a website over time.

Here's my take; DA is a super useful way to quickly state the link authority of a website. For example, if you put a competitor into Link Explorer and see that they've got tons of links from DA80-99 websites, you know that you've got your work cut out. If you do some great content marketing and pick up some links from sites DA60-99, you should get excited, because these will very likely have a positive impact on your site's ranking.

However (and it's a big however), Google itself actually doesn't measure anything like DA. Google looks at the rankability of each *page*, not the entire *domain*. Paul Haahr, one of Google's senior engineers working on search quality, revealed that, rather than looking at the 'Domain Authority' of a website like YouTube, WordPress or Tumblr, for example, Google looks at the authority of the specific user (i.e. the page) on that website. Therefore, being as obsessed with DA as many in the SEO industry are, makes little sense.

The authority of a domain can of course still impact a web page's ranking because links from the homepage to a subpage, for example, still carry weight. Amazon products rank so easily for their target phrases, perhaps not because the Amazon.com *domain* has high authority, but because the pages are so interlinked that the number of links pointing at each product page from other high-authority pages on Amazon is high.

Page Authority (PA)

Page authority is the page-level version of Domain Authority. Just like DA, it rates a page on a scale of one to 100 on its "ranking strength", which is based on the links pointing at that page. This metric is likely to be closer to the one that Google actually measures, although, like DA, it uses a 'best estimate' algorithm to try to mimic Google's own.

Despite this, PA is rarely used. Why? It's simply easier to talk about DA. DA gives any website an easy-to-digest score, whereas PA needs to be measured for every single page.

Trust Flow (TF)

Trust Flow is a metric created by SEO tool Majestic (https://majestic.com), which it defines as: "A score based on quality, on a scale between 0-100. Majestic collated many trusted seed sites based on a manual review of the web. This process forms the foundation of Majestic Trust Flow. Sites closely linked to a trusted seed site can see higher scores, whereas sites that may have some questionable links would see a much lower score."

This metric seeks to predict the trustworthiness of a page based on the trustworthiness of the sites linking to it. In a way, it's not all that different to DA.

Citation Flow (CF)

Citation Flow is another Majestic metric and is defined as: "A score between 0-100 which helps to measure the link equity or "power" the website or link carries. Citation Flow... predicts how influential a URL might be based on how many sites link to it."

How to use these Metrics

DA is treated by almost all of the SEO world as the single most important metric to decide the quality of a link and, in general, it fits that purpose well. It's easier to use than PA, so when we're compiling a list of websites to outreach to, we'll measure their DA and pop it in the spreadsheet so that we can get a quick read on the authority of each website. I'd suggest making DA your default metric, but, like any metric based on estimations, please don't become obsessed about DA, tracking it every week or hunting for only 'high DA' links.

We mostly use CF and TF when we're analysing what sort of links a website has at the start of an SEO campaign. Particularly for websites with lots of links, it's a nice way to see what their current link profile looks like, and that can help us to identify why a site might not be ranking where it should.

Here's the thing, though; whatever the metrics say, the advice is always the same—optimise your website and get high-quality, relevant websites to link to you, then it's almost impossible NOT to improve your ranking.

I repeat, this advice doesn't change, no matter what your DA, PA, CF or TF. If you hate metrics and data, fine, you can safely ignore the lot of them and just *do good promotion*.

Let's now look at some different ways of getting links to your website.

CHAPTER 21

Online Directories

The quickest and easiest source of links for many businesses is directory websites. There are a whole host of free and paid options out there and the best choices for you depend on your market and your business sector. Links from directories won't transform your ranking overnight but, for the time it takes to get your business listed, they're a useful first step.

Having your website listed in directories is useful for three reasons:

1. The links from the directories to your website will increase its authority in Google's eyes and push it up the rankings.

2. If the directories are high-quality and loved by Google (these are the best sort) and your entries are well optimised, then these entries themselves might start ranking high on Google. This has been the case with sites like Yelp, which has historically seen its pages rank quite prominently.

3. Potential customers who somehow end up on the directory website might find your listing and give you a call. This is pretty rare, however, as most generic

business directories provide little business for their members.

The best directories are those that show up in Google when you search for "business directories"! Their prominence on Google is usually a pretty strong indicator that the site is considered high-quality.

You'll notice that most free directory websites offer a paid membership, which usually involves the promise of more exposure and being listed at the top of searches for your category. Don't bother with the paid options, no matter what the sales person says. I'm going to make a confident prediction that you will never see a positive ROI on any paid *generic* directory listing.

Here are some ways to maximise your Google ranking with your directory listings:

- Make sure your descriptions are in-depth and useful to readers by including your target keywords. If you're listing a solicitors firm, for example, mention all the different types of law that they practice to show that the listing is relevant for "divorce law" as well as "probate law" and so on.

- If the directory allows it, add links to your website in the description and use your target keywords as anchor text.

- Make sure that your contact details are *exactly* the same as any contact details you use in your Google Business Profile listing and on your website, if relevant. This then forms what's known as a 'citation' and citations contribute to boosting your map listing's ranking.

- If the directory gives you the option to add pictures and/or videos, opening hours, payment options and the like, add them. Every directory wants its listings to look fully kitted-out, and many will reward listings that have been filled out completely with higher ranking on their sites. It also converts more visitors and makes you stand out from the other generic listings that will likely make up the bulk of the directory.

Market-Specific Directories vs General Directories

Whatever business you are in, there will usually be online directories that are targeted specifically to your market. If you are a local business serving customers in one particular geographic area, you will also find that there are local directories for your area.

In general, listing in these highly-targeted directories is a good idea because they have higher contextual relevance than generic directories. It's also more likely that visitors to niche directories will become qualified leads for you, as they have already narrowed themselves down, either geographically or by interest, to be on the site in the first place.

To find these niche directories, simply Google each of the keywords you're targeting and add the word "directory":

Google accountant directory   🔍

All   Maps   Images   News   Shopping   More   Settings   Tools

About 13,500,000 results (0.31 seconds)

Accountant Directory - find an accountant near you
www.accountant-directory.co.uk/ ▾
Accountant Directory is a comprehensive database of UK accountants and bookkeepers, with information on their training and experience, fees and contact details.

ICAEW Directory of Chartered Accountants: Find Tax services ...
https://find.icaew.com/ ▾
Are you looking for a chartered **accountant** you can trust? The **directory** provided by the ICAEW is the definitive list. Find tax services, bookkeeping, company account preparation services and more.

Find a chartered accountant | About ICAEW | ICAEW
https://www.icaew.com/about-icaew/find-a-chartered-accountant ▾
Browse our online **directory** of firms to find a chartered **accountant**.

Local Accountants Near Me | Find a chartered accountant ...
https://quickbooks.intuit.com/uk/find-an-accountant/ ▾
Find an accountant to help manage your taxes and small business finances from over 10000 UK chartered local **accountants** near me. ... 75% of QuickBooks Online users say working with an **accountant** makes their businesses run better.[1] . Elizabeth loves making ... Want your accountancy listed in our **directory**? Become a ...

Find an advisor - Xero Advisor Directory: Find Accountants ...
https://www.xero.com/uk/advisors/ ▾
Use Xero's advisor **directory** to find a small business accountant, bookkeeper, integrator or financial advisor near you.

Accountants Archive - KashFlow
https://www.kashflow.com/accountant-search/ ▾
Results 1 - 10 of 538 - **Accountant Directory**. We can ensure that you keep your accounts up to date, with software that makes it straightforward to stay in control of the money flowing in and out of your business. Once you've got everything in order, you'll be ready to present your books to an accountant whenever you need to, ...

Local Accountants UK: Find a local accountant
https://www.local-accountants-uk.co.uk/ ▾
Find an account in your county from the specialist UK **Accountants directory**.

Find an ACCA member | ACCA Global
www.accaglobal.com/uk/en/member/find-an-accountant/directory-of-member.html ▾
Choose from the world's best finance and **accounting** professionals. If you need to find a local **accountant** or information on costs and accountancy services, search our register of ACCA members here.

Accountant directory - Clear Books
https://www.clearbooks.co.uk/directory/ ▾
Need to find a Clear Books accountant/bookkeeper? We have made an online **directory** full of the accounting & bookkeeping partners using Clear Books.

Accountant Directory United Kingdom | SearchAccountant
www.searchaccountant.co.uk/ ▾
Search with ease for your local **accountant** in our **directory**. Access tax, **accounting**, audit services and more in your local area.

How to Spot a Spammy Directory

There are plenty of directories that you want absolutely nothing to do with. Back in the SEO dark ages (or glory years, depending on your perspective), getting as many links as possible was the goal and lots of 'SEO directories' sprung up. These were simple websites that anyone could list their business on and, in many cases, they could automate the listing process. This allowed lazy (or efficient, again, depending on your perspective) SEOs to automatically blast out hundreds or even thousands of directory listings in short periods of time.

The trouble is that these directories quickly filled up with irrelevant websites. If you love websites that list viagra suppliers next to Texas roofing companies and Australian fashion boutiques, you would a) be very happy, and b) be almost completely unique. It is pretty easy for Google to spot these sort of junk directories; no new content, very low authority and absolutely no 'topical relevance'.

Listing your website on these directories doesn't necessarily mean that you'll be penalised but it's certainly unlikely to add value. Here are some of the telltale signs of a spammy directory:

- You can see the word "SEO" *anywhere* on the directory.
- The URL of the directory looks unusual e.g. www.directory1423.biz
- The site's main call to action (the primary intended visitor action) is "Submit Link" or "Submit Listing". Good-quality directories are designed primarily for *searchers*, not for the people submitting listings.
- The directory listings are jumbled and there's no attempt to categorise. This makes it useless for visitors.

Most directories that *don't* have a manual review process prior to publishing a listing have been spammed to death, so if you want one overriding rule, it's this; in general, don't list on directories that will put your listing live immediately. The listing should be reviewed first by a human, which keeps the spam out and maintains the integrity of the directory.

Caveat

Directories don't have anywhere near the value they used to, so don't dedicate too much time here. The real link-building winner for our clients is always content marketing (see Chapter 23), but directories are a decent starting point, especially if you're a local business.

CHAPTER 22

Links from video

Another relatively quick way to get links is from videos. If you have a YouTube channel, you can link to your website from your channel page as well as from the descriptions of each of your videos.

Putting links to relevant pages in your video descriptions is a good idea anyway because, if people like what they see in the video, they'd probably like to visit your website to find out more.

The key here is to use the http:// or https:// bit at the start of your link, as this is what's required to make the link clickable on YouTube:

ExposureNinja
Published on Sep 28, 2016

Your page titles are, word-for-word, one of the most important ranking factors on your website. In this quick tip, learn what makes a good page title and discover how to find out if your page titles need some work.

For more free SEO tips, sign up for the free online workshop at
https://www.exposureninja.com/landing...  **Live link**

Category   **Education**

License   **Standard YouTube License**

If you're in YouTube's partner program, you can even add links in your videos themselves.

You don't need to stop at YouTube. Remember that there are lots of video upload sites out there and, whilst YouTube is likely to bring you the lion's share of clicks and views, other video sites like Flickr, Dailymotion, Metacafe, Vimeo and Wistia all have their own audiences and can give you further opportunities to get links from channels and video descriptions.

A little like directories, links from video sites won't transform your ranking in the same way that some great content marketing links might, but they're a quick way to start picking up links and worth getting for the time they take.

Don't have any videos? No problem! You can make simple picture and text videos using a service like Animoto.com. We sometimes make Animoto videos for our clients as part of their marketing campaigns as they're a great way to explain something in an engaging way or act as a companion to a blog post.

CHAPTER 23

Introduction to Content Marketing

We've looked at some quick and simple ways to get links but now we're going to step up into the heavyweight division. Content marketing is an umbrella term that includes a range of strategies which can absolutely transform a website's ranking, from writing blogs to getting featured on some of the world's biggest websites.

In this section, I'm going to share the secrets of our Content Marketing Ninjas here at Exposure Ninja. The strategies and examples you'll read about have been responsible for some frankly unbelievable results, including growing eCommerce sales for one of our clients from less than $500/week to more than $200,000/week (in less than 18 months), getting another client featured live on BBC2 television, doubling SaaS leads in a year, and taking a legal website's leads from 35 per week to more than 100 per *day*.

If the chapters on content marketing whet your appetite, check out our book *The Ultimate Guide To Content Marketing & Digital PR*, written by two of our superstar Ninjas, Charlie and Luke.

Plus, don't forget that if you want some free help and advice on how best to use the strategies in this section, head over to request your free marketing review at https://exposureninja. com/google-book.

CHAPTER 24

How to get Featured on the World's Biggest Websites through Digital PR

For many businesses that have tried traditional PR, either DIY or through a PR company, it involves a lot of payments, a lot of waiting, and then a lot of disappointment. PR is something that many business owners dismiss until they are in 'the big leagues', usually for two reasons:

1. Their image of PR is breakfast television interviews and national newspaper coverage. As a result, they assume it's out of reach.

2. They associate it with highly paid traditional PRs, networking over coffees and inhabiting an impenetrable world of relationships, and without these relationships, it seems impossible to 'break in'.

Unfortunately, these assumptions hold countless businesses back. It's a tragedy. The truth about PR is quite different:

1. It can be very easy to get coverage on a variety of different channels.

2. Savvy businesses can do this for little or no cost at all.

Digital PR is about getting your business featured on the sort of websites that your audience are likely to be reading, whether those are market-specific trade journal websites or national magazines and newspaper sites. We do this for 'visibility', yes, but if you've ever been written up in a newspaper and waited for the 'sales tsunami' only to find it more of a trickle, then you'll know that no-one ever fed their kids on visibility. So, we're also doing it because when these websites link to us, it improves our ranking on Google, whilst also increasing our market's perception and trust of us.

Every day, the editors of the publications your target audience reads stare at half-empty computer screens, wondering how they are going to fill their next issue with good content. Worse, once they finish this month's magazine, today's show or this week's blog posts, the page becomes blank again and they must start from scratch. With shrinking advertising revenue, tight deadlines and a readership with more choice and distraction than ever, the pressure these poor editors face is immense.

This is where you, the savvy marketer or business owner, comes in; the editor's friend and knight in shining armour. Armed with fascinating insights into your industry, current trends and customer needs, you provide the tired, stressed editor with exactly what they want; quality content of interest to their audience. They thank you from the bottom of their heart and tell you that you're welcome back any time to save their bacon again.

If this sounds like wishful fantasy, think again. The perception that PR is a dark, magic art, impossible for those outside the loop, is a creation of those who are selling it, have never tried it, or who tried it and gave up after a few minutes. The reality is that if you've got a good angle, you can get promotional content published in some great publications. The key is to treat it like any other sales job. There is a customer (the editor or journalist) to whom you want to sell your product (your story). You sell to a customer by explaining and demonstrating how your product or service meets their needs, so the process of securing press coverage should be exactly the same.

Once you understand your customer's unmet need, you can create something of value to them and make the sale. The editor's need in this situation is to provide their readers, viewers or subscribers with useful or interesting content in order to increase the likelihood that they'll read, watch or continue their subscription. If you can help them meet this need by providing the useful or interesting information they're after, they will gladly use it.

The approach that *doesn't* work so well is the typical PR approach used by most companies that dabble. They publish press releases with titles like "Company X announces product Y. Now 12% faster and with improved response time..." Boring, overly promotional, valueless *drivel*, which nobody cares about. Even if you manage to find an editor that will print this type of thing, it doesn't get read and it certainly doesn't generate much excitement or interest amongst readers (your ultimate target audience). If your company has released press releases like this in the past, be honest, do you know *anyone* who actually would have wanted to read them, let alone *publish* them?

The most effective adverts focus on the customer and the *benefits* of your product or service, so a press release or article should be no different. The stories with the highest chance of publication are those that provide new insight, recommendations or advice for readers or viewers, a timely survey, or perhaps analysis on a trending topic.

We're not saying you can't talk about your new product or service. Of course there should be a self promotional component, otherwise we are simply freelance writers or interviewees working for free. However, there has to be an angle that is of interest to the audience in order to get the story published and read.

For marketers dipping their toes into PR for the first time, it can be difficult to find an angle for your story that will be interesting and relevant to your target audience. Here are some questions that we use when working with clients to dig out the most interesting nuggets:

- Have you noticed a particular trend in your customers' buying patterns? What are the fashions that are emerging?
- Do you have some recommendations for your audience to avoid some common mistakes, thus positioning your business as the helpful expert?
- If you are announcing a new product, service or business, what sort of interesting stories can you tell about *why* you are launching it or the *need* it serves?

- Is there a large, unmet need which you seek to meet or is there something that posi you perfectly to help a particular type of customer solve this need?

- Do you personally have a story that others would find motivational or inspirational? Careful with this one, though, you've probably noticed that our own stories can be disproportionately fascinating to ourselves.

Once you have chosen your angle, it's time to do some out-reach. Whenever we are getting an article or news item published, we'll draw up a list of suitable outlets and pitch them a slightly different variation of the idea. This allows us to offer each of them exclusivity on that particular story, which dramatically increases the likelihood of it being placed. We'll research and contact the most suitable person, usually by email, sometimes by phone or via social media, offering the story and asking if they think it would be of interest to their readers.

If you have an attractive angle and the editor can see how the readers would find your story interesting, you'll sometimes get a positive response asking you to send over the article. This is when you write the article and send it over. We've found this two-step approach to be much more effective than sending the article cold. The offer of exclusivity is also a differentiator, as these folks are used to being blasted by emails with 100 other poorly-selected contacts in the CC: line.

Once an editor has requested your article, write the article properly and prepare it in a way that fits with the style of the publication. Use a similar word count and language to other published articles to minimise the editing that they have to do. If you send over a half-finished piece that requires extensive rewriting, it's far less appealing than a ready-to-publish article. If it needs to be proofread, then hire a proofreader. Give it your very best shot and work as if it really matters. Trust us, it won't go unnoticed with the editor.

If you're writing for a magazine or newspaper, try to include an image that they can use alongside the story. Where possible, it should be original, because this eliminates any copyright or licensing issues. If you have to use a stock photo, make sure that it's licensed for use. Remember that the aim here is to make publishing your article an extremely simple and desirable proposition. The less work you require the publication to do (including sourcing a suitable picture), the greater the chance that they'll run the piece.

While we're on the topic of PR, I wanted to share a strategy that you need to know about that can be a useful source of leads. The following section is taken from our book, *101 Ways to Get More Customers from the Internet*. While it's not strictly SEO-related, it is *very* profitable, so we wanted to include it here:

Using PR For Free Advertising/Lead Generation

We have built two entire businesses on the back of lead generation campaigns run through articles written for magazines. The articles provide insight or advice about a particular subject of interest to the reader, then offer a free gift to readers. They are invited to text or visit a website to claim their free gift and we then use these contact details to market to them. The free gift itself is usually a piece of promotional material with enough valuable information contained in it for it to have high perceived value.

To give an example, after the success of Ben the plasterer, I started building a lot of websites for tradesmen. The marketing funnel here was:

- Article written in a trade magazine read by my target audience (e.g. *Plumbing Heating and Air Movement Monthly*).
- The article would be called something like "5 Ways to Increase Your Website's Leads" and would give readers some great tips to increase their website's visibility.
- At the end of the article, I'd offer readers a free DVD (remember those?) which showed them the things I was talking about live on the screen. To get the DVD, they just had to text their address to a phone number.
- This DVD would pitch our website service and that's how we'd sell the websites.

This was basically free advertising, as these magazines were delivered right to my target audience. Rather than paying an ad fee, I just wrote a killer article. They let me keep in the mention of the DVD because that was super useful for readers too. I could tell when the magazines started hitting doorsteps because my phone would temporarily become unusable.

Depending on the magazine, I'd get 100-200 texts from tradesmen asking for DVDs over a couple of days.

By using press in this way, you can get highly effective advertising, free of charge, disguised as articles. The quality of the articles is so high that they attract readers and, by offering a tantalising offer at the end, we're making sure that we motivate the readers to take action (i.e giving us their contact details).

Of course, some publications will smell a rat with this approach and see that you're just sneaking in some free advertising under the radar. Like anything, it's a numbers game. Many won't, though, particularly the publications in very niche markets, and they'll happily run your ads free of charge. Ads? Did I say ads? I meant articles.

For those who do protest at your inclusion of an offer, you can strike a deal to run a paid advert as well, in return for the article's inclusion. Don't fall for the 'minimum of five insertions' rule to 'build familiarity' but instead tell the magazine that you're testing the effectiveness of the ad using a lead generation offer, so you'll immediately be able to gauge the response rate.

Pitching for TV Coverage

If you're aiming for TV or online video coverage, do everything you can to show your contact that you'd make a good interviewee. Send a short and well-lit video of yourself in front of the camera appearing comfortable and relaxed (as the Covid-19 pandemic has made webcam calls the norm, this is more important than ever). Make sure you know what you're going to be talking about and your lines are rehearsed enough so that they sound natural, then you can focus more on the delivery than what you're actually saying. To make the most of any TV appearances you get, make sure to do whatever you can to get a link from the show's website, as the authority and quality of these sites tend to be very good.

Following up Journalists and Editors

The folks receiving articles and emails for press coverage tend to be extremely busy and deluged with emails, so it's a good idea to send a follow-up after a couple of working days if you haven't heard back from them. Politely ask if they received your work and if they had any feedback as to whether it would be the sort of thing their audience would be interested in. We find that it's almost always *only through the follow up* that we get a response from the editor, so it's important to be diligent about it.

Thank anyone who offers to run the piece, *because people hardly ever say thank you.* This is also a great opportunity to let the editor or writer know that you've had a fantastic response from the article and that lots of readers have been in touch with questions. In fact, you noticed that most people were asking the same four questions, so *"I've written a follow-up article which answers these questions and gives readers some additional tips, based on what they seem to be struggling with the most. Would you be interested in me sending this over...?"*

CHAPTER 25

95% of Surveys are run by Businesses looking for PR

Contributing to the news is one thing; creating the news is something else entirely.

In early 2017, the Daily Mail warned readers that the world is facing a "global epidemic of blindness". Skim past the fear-inducing fluff that the Mail is famous for and it turns out that the headline is from a single report by a Spanish researcher.

A little further down the page—surprise, surprise—we learn that the very same Spanish researcher just so happens to have developed a new light filter product to protect us all from the blindness epidemic. What are the chances?

It's easy to scoff at reports, studies and surveys, but this particular marketing strategy has stood the test of time. An authoritative newspaper and some sciencey-sounding statistics combine to make an irresistible sales pitch. Remember the bad old days when "More Doctors Smoke Camels Than Any Other Cigarette"?

Think that running surveys like this is beyond your business? It's absolutely not. Google Surveys (https://marketingplatform. google.com/about/surveys) and Survey Monkey (www.survey monkey.com) are two examples of websites that will do the hard work of finding and weighting responses for you. You can get statistically representative responses to a question in less than two weeks.

This tactic, known as "data outreach" by the Ninjas here at Exposure Ninja, is simple to execute and we're going to share exactly how we do it. Use the internet to produce some cheap but meaningful data, then reach out to websites and influencers who might share that data.

To show what this looks like, here are a few examples of massively successful surveys that we've run for clients big and small:

eCommerce Data Outreach Example

eCommerce businesses can produce interesting survey data by reporting on trends and public attitudes to particular products. For one of our clients, we ran a survey asking the public what they thought of the health benefits and risks of e-cigarettes. We organised the survey through YouGov, who put our questions to over 2,000 members of the public. We published the results on our client's blog.

The study got picked up by 266 different publications, with a total audience of over 80 million people. Each time someone reported on our data, they linked back to the original blog post.

As a link acquisition strategy, this ranked as one of our best campaigns of all time when we calculate hours worked versus backlinks earned!

Lead Generation Data Outreach

Another client of ours identifies people who need legal help and sells these leads to law firms. Their most lucrative market is mis-sold PPI, a competitive market where they were up against some very well-funded competitors.

The government announced a deadline for all PPI claims and the Financial Conduct Authority launched a huge advertising campaign featuring Arnold Schwarzenegger to promote it. We waited a couple of months, then conducted a study to see how effective this ad campaign had actually been at educating the public on the PPI deadline.

We surveyed over 800 people and found that, actually, only 16% knew when the deadline was, despite the shed load of money spent on Arnie's ads! This story was picked up by hundreds of websites including the Mirror, Unilad and Yahoo Finance, all providing very high-authority links to the original data on our client's blog.

This graph shows what happened to their lead volume over time, as we repeatedly implemented this strategy:

By piggybacking on a current news story and providing data that proved our point, we were able to earn the kind of coverage that's normally reserved for much larger businesses. The graph shows the website's growth from around 10 leads per day to almost 200.

How to Run your Own Data Outreach Study

The secret to running a study that picks up attention is being interesting. When creating your survey questions, try thinking of the headline you'd like to produce. Headlines have to be sensational, or at least surprising. A survey that tells us something we already know isn't going anywhere fast.

Before building a study, think about any existing data your business might have built up over the years. Something that might seem boring to you, such as the price of spare car parts over the last decade, can form the basis of an exciting news story about the soaring costs of motoring, for example.

Another shortcut is commenting on an existing survey that never got the attention it deserved. The wonks at the Office For

National Statistics (www.ons.gov.uk) produce well-researched statistical reports that absolutely nobody reads. However, if you're a real-estate agent, for example, I'm sure you could add an expert comment to one of their deep dives into property prices by region that suddenly makes the story pop.

If you'd like to build your own survey from scratch, here are the basic steps:

1. Think of the headline that you'd like to generate.
2. Is the headline related to a current trend and your area of expertise? If so, continue.
3. Think of a question you could ask the public that could create that headline.
4. Consider targeting your survey by demographics (location, sex, age, etc.)
5. Run a test survey in the office with a couple of mates. Fix any errors you uncover!
6. Use Google Surveys or YouGov to get your survey results.
7. While you're waiting for the results to come in, identify journalists who you can pitch to.
8. The results are in! Write up a blog that analyses the results.
9. If you have a designer, ask them to make your dry data into something beautiful. Infographics can be a great way of collecting links.
10. Send the results to the press, both via individual journalist pitches and a formal press release.

When deciding between a cheap option like Google Surveys and an external polling service like YouGov, it's important to consider how "sciencey" your results need to be. In general, if you're after an opinion on a superficial topic, nobody will mind if your research is a bit rough around the edges. If you're asking a "Your Money or Your Life" question that might influence people to take financial and/or health actions, consider spending a little extra on a professional survey company.

When you have the data, compile it into a blog post and put it on your website, with a catchy headline. The aim is to make something shareworthy here. It needs to be simple, surprising and worth talking about. A little further into your blog, when all the casual readers have dropped off, you can include the geeky info about how you conducted the survey, the number of respondents and so on.

Next, you'll need to promote your study. There are a few ways that you can do this, from reaching out to journalists and editors personally to paying a PR firm (be careful) to promote the study results for you.

Press release distribution services can be a useful tool here, as they'll send your story to lots of news outlets. If it's interesting enough, these news outlets will run the story. If you've never written a press release before, use Google "press release template" or contact Exposure Ninja for some help. Journalists can be a bit snobby about press releases so make sure you've got your formatting right.

Remember that a press release is just an advert. The mistake that people make is in thinking that it's an advert for your *business*. It's not; it's an advert for your *story*. The goal is to get journalists to publish the *story*, not buy from your company.

CHAPTER 26

Blogger and Influencer Outreach

If you sell a product that people love talking about, blogger and influencer outreach can be a great way to get attention and links.

For the relaunch of a previously popular beer, we were brought on board to build awareness of the brand and the rebirth, whilst bringing it to the attention of a younger audience and making it a bit 'cooler' than it had previously been seen. There was also a large stock on Amazon that was slowly going out of date and this needed shifting, so we had a very tangible goal too! We thought this was a great opportunity to kill two birds with one beer bottle, so we planned a blogger and influencer campaign to do both.

In the run up to Christmas, we contacted lots of mummy bloggers to let them know that we had something which would be perfect for their Christmas gift guides (even if they didn't plan to run a Christmas gift guide yet.). We offered to send them some beer so that they or their husbands could try it out and see if it'd be a suitable inclusion in their gift guide. It usually was, so they wrote about the beer in their Christmas gift guides, which tended to be some of the most popular posts amongst their blog readers. The links in their posts directed visitors to the brand's website for more information and to Amazon to buy online immediately.

By doing this, the beer brand appeared in front of their target audience in a way that was far more authoritative than, for example, running magazine or radio ads. The blogger was someone who their readers really respected and they were just giving an honest review of a product that they loved, then sending visitors straight onto Amazon to buy it. According to a Hubspot study, 75% of people don't accept advertising as 'the truth' but 71% say they are more likely to buy something if they're referred to it from social media.

We didn't limit our outreach to mummy bloggers, though. We also targeted vegan bloggers, foodie bloggers and male bloggers (the beer brand's target audience was predominantly male). In most cases, we offered some free products if they wanted to write a review. As a result of this strategy, we sold out of the Amazon stock before Christmas and had to stop the promotions.

Is this strategy right for every business? Absolutely not. If you're selling radiator valves, for example, it could be tricky to find influential bloggers eager to write long, passionate reviews and add your products to gift guides. That's okay, because digital PR outreach to industry publications would be much more effective for you. Each of these techniques are all just different flavours of content marketing, and you'll find the particular strings that work best for your business and your audience.

Let's assume for now, though, that influencers are likely to want to talk about what you sell. Let's look at how to run a campaign.

First, you'll start by creating a list of bloggers and/or influencers who are likely to have a target audience which matches your ideal customer. For example, if you sell children's clothing, then you'll want to target mummy bloggers, since readers of mummy blogs are often other parents. If you sell fitness products, then fitness influencers and personal trainers will obviously be a good fit for you.

We've written extensively about how to find influencers that will make tectonic movements for your brand in our book *The Ultimate Guide To Content Marketing & Digital PR*. That goes beyond the scope of this book, but you can find influencers through Google searches and on social media platforms.

At this point, if you're not already on Instagram, Facebook and YouTube, reading blogs and spending time consuming influencer content in your market, it's a good idea to start. Without understanding how your subculture works online, you risk coming across like an outsider or missing the mark with your outreach and targeting. Spend time getting to know your influencer landscape, understanding who the 'super influencers' with huge followings are and who have smaller audiences but perhaps greater engagement. Also, notice how often these bloggers and influencers are posting about products.

This is a great time to address one of the most common misconceptions about influencer outreach. That is, in order to be an 'influencer', you must be a Kendall Jenner level social monster, with millions of fans on every platform and each post getting tens of thousands of comments.

Not only are these guys almost always out of reach and *super* overpriced (a 2017 Mediakix study [https://mediakix.com/blog/highest-paid-celebrities-endorsement-rates-on-instagram] claimed that Beyoncé commanded up to $1 million per Insta-gram post that year), they're unlikely to blog (and link) to you and their audience is so wide that the percentage of followers that are likely to be a good fit for your products is super small. The term 'micro influencer' is usually used to describe people with 10,000 to 100,000 followers and who, according to a 2016 Markerly study (https://markerly.com/blog/instagram-marketing-does-influencer-size-matter), generate significantly more interactions *per follower* than the Beyonce and Kardashian-level influencers.

For the purposes of SEO, you really want to focus on targeting influencers that have their own blogs, as this will be how you get the links to increase your website's authority. So, aside from reader numbers and looking at the number of comments each post gets, the other metric that you can track when you're choosing influencers is the Domain Authority of their blog. As we said earlier, Domain Authority isn't a perfect metric, but it will give you an indication of how valuable a link from this person's website might be.

CHAPTER 27

How to get Influencers to Promote your Business

The key to getting influencers to talk about your products is offering tasty bait. How can you create a win-win offer? Here are some ways you can sweeten the deal:

<u>Send a free product</u>

Send the influencer a free product (and make sure you cover postage!) or invite them in to try out a service (such as a haircut, a teeth-whitening treatment, a restaurant meal, or a hotel stay). For micro-influencers, this may be enough, especially if the product or service is a good one.

Note that "product samples" (products you send out but expect the influencer to return) are less tempting. Not only do they not get to keep a product but they also have the hassle of returning it. If possible, give them something they can keep.

<u>Send many free products</u>

If your products are low-ticket items, such as health food supplements or protein bars, send influencers a hamper. You can even involve other related brands with this and work together if you're ambitious. An influencer probably isn't going to write a blog post for just one sachet of protein powder, for example.

Suggest content ideas in your pitch

Like editors, bloggers and influencers are busy. Most smaller influencers have a full-time job completely unrelated to their blog and social media work. They won't always have time to brainstorm ideas about how to feature your products. If you sell peanut butter, suggest peanut butter recipes. If Christmas or Valentine's is coming up, suggest that they include your product in a gift guide. Provide the influencer with photos to use as well, the less work they have to do, the more tempting the offer is.

Send them a free product *and* an extra one to giveaway to their audience

This is a sweeter deal for you and the influencer. Giveaways engage readers/followers much more than product reviews. Use contests to increase your own social followers and/or website visits using a tool like Rafflecopter. If this is a giveaway hosted on social media, you may consider providing the influencer with a budget to boost the post to maximise its reach and engagement.

Set up an affiliate link scheme

Provide the influencer with affiliate links so they can earn a small commission on every sale you make through their links. Many hotel booking websites use this tactic.

Give them exclusive discount codes for their followers

Provide exclusive discount codes or similar deals for the influencer's followers. If possible, use a unique code for each influencer. This makes the influencer feel special and it allows you to track sales.

Share the influencer's post on your social media

If your business has good social media followings and engagement, you can promise to share the influencer's social posts on your own accounts, too. The influencer may appreciate the cross-promotion and you can show off the influencer who's testing out your products. Third party validation never hurt anyone's sales!

Invite the influencer to an event

Put on an event for influencers where they can sample your product or see your restaurant/hotel, etc. These work particularly well for big brands and location-based businesses based in areas where there is a high density of relevant influencers (e.g. big cities).

Invite them to join your community of influencers

Invite your influencers to join an exclusive influencer community via a Facebook group. This helps you organise the influencers that you're working with and re-engage them easily at a later date for a new campaign. It's also a chance to flatter the influencers and make them feel like an important part of your campaign, rather than an afterthought.

Consider offering the influencer a brand ambassadorship

Consider asking an influencer to be an 'ambassador' for your brand. A brand ambassador is an influencer in a long-term agreement with a business. They will promote a company regularly in exchange for exclusive access to new products and services. Larger influencers can become well-paid brand ambassadors—think celebrity sponsorship. I'd always suggest working with the influencer on a smaller scale before setting up a long-term arrangement like this, though.

How to Pitch to Influencers without Feeling Awkward

When you pitch to influencers, be upfront about what you're offering and what you'd like in return. Influencers get endless streams of pitches from businesses (often terrible, vague template emails that they ignore) so cut the crap and tell them what you want. We've worked with thousands of bloggers and influencers and many of our Ninjas are influencers both inside and outside of work. We know from personal experience that playing coy is not the way to go in these pitches.

Our focus in this book is improving your website's organic ranking. Many businesses work with influencers as a brand awareness or social media building exercise. However, if you're gunning for better rankings, you want to focus on building backlinks to your website. This means predominantly looking for influencers who have blogs with a good Domain Authority and who write content in a niche relevant to your business.

When you're pitching to influencers, let them know exactly what you want to get out of the collaboration. If you want your product featured or reviewed on their blog, then get confirmation of this via email upfront. You might agree on more social posts or other promotions with them on top of this, depending on the influencer.

CHAPTER 28

How to use Inbound PR requests

The strategies in this section can (and will, if you follow them) get literally anyone into some of the world's largest publications, so long as you can pitch yourself as an expert at something.

Journalists who write for large publications (magazines like Forbes, national newspapers, etc.) are very busy people. They have tight deadlines, don't get paid enough for their work and want to write the best pieces they possibly can. Many of them are freelance, so they write for other publications too, and will need to write about a diverse range of topics. This puts them under a lot of pressure. Luckily, these journos have us, the friendly and helpful marketers, to help them out.

Imagine a journalist is approaching a deadline to submit an article about 'National Heart Month', for example. Chances are that they won't personally know too many experts on heart health to mention in their article. What they might do is use a journalist enquiry service like ResponseSource.com or HARO (Help A Reporter Out – check out episode 93 of the Exposure Ninja podcast [https://exposureninja.com/podcast/93] where I interview Peter Shankman, its founder).

Journalist enquiry services like these allow journalists to blast an enquiry out to a database of subscribers (that's you and I) who might be able to give them an expert quote to use in their articles. In return, you get featured in the article and will get a link from it to your website. Seen those fish that live on the sharks, keeping them clean by eating the bugs and stuff? That's the type of relationship that you and I can have with journalists from some of the world's biggest publications. Although, in that example, they're the mighty sharks and we're the scum-eating leech bugs, but hey, marketers do what marketers gotta do.

So how do journalist enquiry services work? I'm going to explain the paid options and then I'm going to explain how you don't really have to do any of this and can just use Twitter instead.

When you sign up for a service like Response Source (www.responsesource.com), you'll choose the categories that you want to receive enquiries in; for example, 'Business and Finance', 'Food and Drink' or 'Motoring'. Each category has its own annual price and a subscription gets you on the list for all enquiries in that category. Once you are subscribed, you'll receive email enquiries that look like this:

Media outlet: PRIMA [1] (Spokesperson or expert)
Media outlet website: www.prima.co.uk [2]
Freelance journalist: FIONA FORD
JournalistDirectory Profile:
http://www.journalistdirectory.com/journalist/XmmXE/Fiona-Ford?ref=grs
[3]
Media type: Consumer media
Deadline for leads: 14 Apr 2015 16:00

ENQUIRY SHORT SUMMARY
Tips for relaxation

QUERY
Hi all,
Writing a piece on how to relax over the summer and looking for tips
and suggestions women from 30 and above can relate to.
I'm after anything and everything so whether it's scheduling time to
meditate, getting a great night's sleep, lowering blood pressure - I'm
open to all ideas but would love to hear from you.

As ever we can plug websites, contacts, campaigns etc so please do get
in touch if you're interested.

All best,

Fiona

HOW TO REPLY
Email: rs-QQLXEL.TAgLz@email.responsesource.com
Twitter: @fionajourno [4]

MEDIA OUTLET DESCRIPTION
"Prima is a mass-market general-interest women's monthly magazine.
Features advice on health, wellbeing and fashion as well as family and
consumer issues, along with ideas to inspire home-makers who look for
value-for-money solutions."

ISSUE DATE*: August

From this enquiry, you can see the publication (Prima in this
case), the name of the journalist and a link to her profile. You'll
see that she's a freelancer, which means she writes for other
publications. A successful contribution could lead to features in
other places too, which could equal more high-quality links. The

deadline given is a very strict one, so strict, in fact, that if you email *after* this deadline, the emails will actually bounce!

Notice how, in the query, it also says, "as ever we can plug websites, contacts, campaigns etc...". This means we'll get a link.

You'll also see the journalist's Twitter handle: @fionajourno. One of the few super valuable uses for Twitter is outreach, as it's the social network used most frequently by journalists. Follow them, like their posts and contribute when you can. More on how to do that shortly.

Let's look at what to do when you get an enquiry which is right for your business from a journalist enquiry service. Remember that this is a sales activity like any other, so the first thing you want to do is to understand the prospect. This journalist is busy, time-pressured and about to be deluged with 200 emails from people just like you. So, sending them an email that says "Hi Fiona, I'd love to contribute. Could you tell me a little bit more?" will get about as much response as writing to Google and asking for ranking.

You want to give this person everything they need, as concisely as possible and as fast as possible. Imagine yourself as a gourmet chef, preparing an irresistible bite-sized meal that your patrons can't help but sample. Here's an excellent response to a journalist enquiry, written by one of our Ninjas, Luke (he's a content marketing genius). Feel free to swipe and deploy at will:

Hi Fiona,

I represent Peter Lemon, an experienced personal trainer. He has the following relaxation tips:

"There's a widespread misconception that suggests in order to relax, you have to rest. Actually, physical exercise brings about amazing feelings of relaxation. This is because exercise is key to reducing the body's stress hormones, notably adrenaline and cortisol. Just as importantly, exercise is linked with the production of 'feel-good' endorphins, the body's natural painkillers and mood boosters. All forms of exercise can help you beat stress, with yoga being particularly effective due to the stretching and deep-breathing exercises."

If you found the information useful, you can give credit to:

Peter Lemon, expert personal trainer and founder of the Academy of Fitness Professionals, a specialist training academy offering certified, industry recognised fitness courses in the UK.

All the best,

Luke

Notice how we give the entire tip *and* the bio *and* the link that the journalist can use, if they choose? The other key here was speed. Do we get these tips approved by the client? Rarely, because time is of the essence and if we wait six hours for a busy business owner to write a tip, Fiona has already had fifty tips.

This stuff works. Here's a link that this strategy secured, for this exact client:

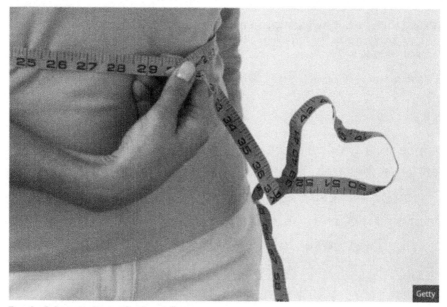

Exercise is important to combat heart disease

Being overweight increases your risk of developing heart disease, but your body shape can have an impact too. "People who carry weight on their waistline are more vulnerable to heart disease than those that carry it on their hips," says health expert and personal trainer Peter Lemon. "That's why exercise is extremely important when it comes to reducing the risk of heart disease."

That's a link from the Mirror, which has a Domain Authority of 91. This type of visibility also leads to greater opportunities.

One day, a BBC researcher was looking around online for a health expert to come on Victoria Derbyshire's show and talk about the health implications of those 'waist trainer corsets'. They found an article we had written for this client, on that topic, and got in touch to see if Peter (the client) was available to come onto the show. They picked him up, took him to television centre, and he was live on TV:

This type of coverage is self-perpetuating. As you get featured in more high-authority places, it gives you credibility that you can use in future pitches, opening doors to greater and greater opportunities.

How to do all of this without Paying for Journalist Enquiry Services

Journalist enquiry services are great and can get you some awesome links. However, if you don't fancy shelling out hundreds or even thousands of moolah just to subscribe, the good news is that you don't need to.

There are two Twitter hashtags that you can follow instead: #journorequest (twitter.com/search?q=%23journorequest) and #prrequest (twitter.com/search?q=%23prrequest). Here's an example:

This tweet could apply to every single business owner reading this book. A quick Google can give you an opinion on the tax changes and away you go. Why might we want to reach out to Lizzy?

Elizabeth Anderson ✔
@lizzyandersonuk

Business reporter at the Telegraph, particularly interested in enterprise and innovation

Oh, that's right, because she's a *business reporter at the Telegraph*, Domain Authority 96.

Here's another example:

What do entrepreneurs wear for work? Again, every single business owner on the planet could have an opinion on this. Alison writes for Forbes, so I decided to send something over:

She emailed, I replied quickly with a quote. Five days later...

Alison Coleman @alisonbcoleman · Mar 21

How You Dress For Work Can Make You
More Productive? via @forbes
forbes.com/sites/alisonco ... thnx
@ExposureNinja @claireehowell @CerubPR

      ↩   ♺ 5   ♥ 8   ●●●   View summary

Great! She tweeted Exposure Ninja and a link to the article she had written:

Forbes / Entrepreneurs

The Little Black Book (

MAR 20, 2016 @ 08:37 AM   2,485 VIEWS

Does Your Choice Of Work Outfit Make You More Productive?

Mark Zuckerberg swears by wearing the same casual clothes to work every day because it allows him to focus on more important decisions, while wearing jeans all the time never did Steve Jobs any harm. Richard Branson refuses to wear a necktie, a symbol of formality, but it hasn't stopped people from wanting to do business with him.

Alison Coleman
CONTRIBUTOR

I write about entrepreneurs, in particular, the disruptive ones

But does your choice of working day outfit make you more productive? Although entrepreneur Tim Kitchen mainly runs his 45-person digital marketing firm Exposure Ninja from his home office, he still dresses sharply in shirt and trousers.

He says: "Meeting with clients and staff over Skype and filming videos is all part of a day's work, so looking professional is as important as it would be in an office. Having said that, if I've finished meetings for the day and the sun is hitting the balcony, there's nothing wrong with a bit of shorts and t-shirt working on the laptop."

But whether the team is working from their home offices or out meeting clients face to face, they avoid wearing suits for fear of alienating their often casually dressed SMB clients.

Notice how Zuck, Branson and Jobs have to share one paragraph, whilst I and Exposure Ninja get three, plus a link from Forbes? You can do this—anyone can do this.

Sidenote, see how I was running a "45-person digital marketing firm" back in 2016? Today, we have over 100+ happy Ninjas working 100% remotely around the world. Remarkable, eh?

Some quick tips before you head to Twitter to go and search for #journorequests:

- Be speedy. You usually need to reply within at least a couple of hours. We have Content Marketing Ninjas here at Exposure Ninja who spend time scouring online for juicy opportunities, so you'll want to check in at least twice per day on Twitter if you don't have someone who can do this for you (i.e. Exposure Ninja!).

- If you're busy, have a look at who the journalist writes for before you respond. It doesn't take *loads* of work to get featured but, even so, there are people out there who tweet out using #journorequest and #prrequest for all sorts of rubbish websites.

- Give the journalist an angle that makes their story more interesting by finding the part of your opinion on the topic which is most likely to be of interest. Would Alison have published my "dressed up despite working from home" piece if I'd have just tweeted "I wear normal clothes"? Of course not. I wanted to give her something unusual and that piqued her interest.

We've used these hashtags to get featured in all sorts of places: Forbes, The Guardian, The Telegraph, Inc..., all with links to ours and clients' websites. If your competitors aren't doing this (clue – they almost certainly aren't), it's a great way to build your website's authority over them by another level.

CHAPTER 29

Using Social Media to Boost your SEO

Back in December 2010, Google's Matt Cutts announced that Google *does* measure links on Facebook and Twitter in its ranking algorithm. In fact, the Google engineers were working on understanding the authority of social profiles in order to weigh these links.

However, fast forward to 2014 and Google's stance changed. Matt announced in another video that social signals do *not* impact ranking. What caused this shift? Is Google telling the truth and, if it is, does social really have no impact on ranking?

The stated reason for the shift is that because social pages change frequently, Google can't be confident that the content of a page is going to be up to date or accurate at some point in the future. In the announcement, Matt also mentioned that, because Google had been previously blocked from crawling Facebook, the Google team was wary of building tools to measure authority, in case they were blocked again.

Is it possible that Google is stretching the truth? Perhaps. Google clearly indexes and serves tweets in search results, almost in real time. So it clearly has the crawl capacity and speed to be able to use social signals in ranking, if it chooses. Heck, if it was doing so in 2010, surely it would be today, right? A lot of SEOs believe that social signals *are* used in ranking, as there is a correlation between social shares of particular pages and those pages' prominent ranking. It has also been suggested, however, that this is correlation *not* causation. The best content gets shared a lot *and* it ranks well; those things don't necessarily have to be connected. Our own suspicions are that Googlebot crawls social channels to look for links, although just because they're being crawled doesn't mean they'll rank.

So, does Google use social signals to influence ranking or not? The jury's out and there's no conclusive proof either way. Here's your plan, then:

- Optimise all of your social media pages
- Build your authority on every platform that you use
- Write and share amazing content
- Don't expect social to have any impact on your ranking

That last point is key. So many businesses plough so much time into social media hoping for all sorts of benefits, few of which materialise.

Some of our most successful and profitable SEO clients have fewer than 1,000 Facebook likes and almost no interaction across any of their social channels. To look at their businesses on Facebook, you'd think that the company was dead, but it doesn't matter *at all* to their success because they're targeting searchers, not people on Facebook. Other successful SEO clients have thriving social channels and generate significant proportions of their sales through Facebook, Instagram and Twitter but that's not the cause of their SEO success!

Our book *Profitable Social Media Marketing* lifts the lid on some of the world's most profitable social media marketing campaigns, so, in the interest of keeping this book focused purely on SEO, in this section we'll look only at the ways to maximise your *ranking* using social.

Optimise your Social Profiles

Whatever your business, you should have profiles on Facebook, Twitter, Instagram, Google Business Profile (formerly *Google My Business*), LinkedIn and YouTube. Each of these channels gives you an indexable 'homepage' with the ability to add descriptions and links.

Optimising your social media profiles is similar to optimising directory listings. The key things to think about are:

- Complete listings. Add profile photos, descriptive text about the business, and make sure that the profile looks 'finished'.

- Keyword usage. Use the keywords that you want to target in your description. This is good SEO practice and it can also get your profiles found by searchers on each network looking for people doing what you do.

- Keep active on each channel. If you haven't posted in a year, not only does it look bad to any search engine that may or may not crawl your profile, but it looks bad to *humans* who want to look you up.

- Link to your website from your social pages. As well as linking from the 'website link' field that most social networks allow you to use, you can sometimes use links from your business description.

How to get your Business Showing Up as an Expanded Listing on Google

If you haven't already, you absolutely need to sign up and claim your Google Business Profile (formerly *Google My Business*) at www.google.com/business. This will help you to control the information that shows up when people Google your business name:

This type of expanded listing is more likely to show for your business if you have your Google Business Profile page set up, with your other social profiles optimised.

We're often contacted by owners of websites that have suffered from negative reviews or trash talk on forums, either from previous customers or naughty competitors. Sometimes, these websites rank prominently for the business name, so having your expanded Google Business Profile listing dominate the search page can be a good way to present your company in a more positive light.

Optimising your Facebook Page

First, make sure that you have a properly set up Facebook *Business* page, rather than just a personal profile. If you don't have a business page yet, go to facebook.com/pages/create and follow the instructions to get one set up.

As we said before, completing your profile is absolutely key. In the description or 'story' space of your Facebook page, you want to explain clearly to Google (and to visitors) what your business does, using the keywords that they're likely to have used to find it. You'll also want to demonstrate that you're reliable and trustworthy by picking up lots of positive reviews. You'll notice from the screenshot above that Google *is* indexing Facebook's reviews of your business, so getting positive reviews on Facebook, as well as Google, is important.

How to get Lots of Reviews on Facebook and Google

Firstly, a couple of universal truths:

1. Getting reviews is a pain; a pain for you and a pain for your customers. It's *never* easy.

2. The percentage of people you ask for a review who will actually give you one is tiny. People are busy and generally lazy. Besides, most don't care about your business enough to try to help you grow. It's only as brutal as it's accurate.

With those truths in mind, the only way to consistently pick up more reviews than your competitors is to completely automate the process. If you rely on manually asking each person for a review, you're doomed to fail, as you'll get disheartened after five heartfelt requests bring in zero reviews. However, if you have an automated follow-up email which goes out each time someone buys from you and includes a link to submit a review, then eventually you'll start to see your reviews tick up.

If you request your free website and marketing review from https://exposureninja.com/google-book, you'll notice that, along with the video we record for you, we'll send you the link to our Facebook or Google review section to ask you for a review of the service. This is automatic so nobody has to think about asking and our review count continues to tick up.

You might be tempted to buy reviews from third party sites. I'll tell you three things about this strategy:

1. **It works.** We see some of our clients' competitors buying reviews and it's very frustrating for the client. At the time of writing, TripAdvisor is the worst in this regard, as they seem not to care.

2. **It won't work forever.** As these companies develop more sophisticated 'fake review detection' algorithms, the junk *will* be weeded out and the reviews will disappear.

3. **It's usually pretty obvious that you're doing it.** Fake reviews tend to come from fake profiles that only leave wildly positive or negative reviews and who review geographically diverse businesses. If your potential customers spot this, it's really not a good look.

Despite its effectiveness, then, fake reviews are not something that we'd recommend. It's actually genuinely easier to build a successful business by doing something well enough that you get good reviews, and to then automate the collection of them, than it is to blag your way to the top.

One super awesome tip that our Head of Marketing, Dale Davies, has for brick and mortar businesses is to put a sign up in your location, which not only lists the WiFi password, but also displays a nice "please leave us a review on Google" message with a shortened URL that customers can copy. You might be surprised to see how many of your customers leave you reviews whilst they wait for their appointments.

This completes the offsite promotion section of this book and you now know how to get links from directories, videos, digital PR, original data outreach, bloggers and influencers, journalist enquiry services, Twitter, and your own social media profiles. Blimey! Using all of these tools will give you the sort of visibility and mentions that will lead to market dominating rankings.

SECTION 4

Designing and Implementing your SEO Strategy

Now you know everything that you *can* do to get to the top of Google. You might feel a sense of calm clarity (unlikely), or, you might be feeling an overwhelming sense of panic (more likely).

The truth is that no single human on earth has the time to do everything in this book, let alone business owners or marketing managers that already have other stuff to do. That's completely okay. In this section, we're going to design a plan to help you identify and *focus* on the things that are going to move the needle the most for you.

I'm also going to give you some counterintuitive advice about what to do if you're thinking of hiring help.

CHAPTER 30

How to plan an SEO strategy

The best SEO campaigns focus on low-hanging fruit first. This book is laid out in the order it is for a reason. First, you need to get your website together. Then, and only then, start thinking about links and promotion.

To make it super simple, I'm now going to explain the priorities that we run through when we're working on a client SEO campaign so that you can work through these same priorities for yourself. When we start working with a client, our goal is to show a ranking improvement as quickly as possible. It's likely that this is your goal, too.

If you'd like us to recommend *your* top SEO priorities, then request a free SEO and marketing review at https://exposure ninja.com/review and we'll point out the areas that you should focus on first to deliver the fastest results. We'll record a video that analyses your website, SEO and competition and we'll give you a prioritised action plan at the end, which you can follow to hit your 12-month sales targets.

Additionally, I created a marketing priority system last year called the 90-Minute Marketing Masterplan, which you can get for free at https://exposureninja.com/90.

The 90-Minute Marketing Masterplan will help you take all of the things you could be working on to improve your website's ranking, traffic, leads and sales and sort them into a priority order based on which tasks will increase your business' revenue.

It's a combo of a video course and spreadsheet system, so make sure you claim a copy.

Step 1: Website Review

Before doing any SEO, it's a good idea to analyse the suitability of your website. The following things are all going to be crucial to the success of your SEO campaign, so if any of these aren't in place, fixing them is the first place to start:

- Is the website mobile friendly?
- Does the site have separate pages targeting each of your main product or service areas?
- Does each page have at least 300 words of text copy? This is a simplistic but useful definition of 'enough text copy'.
- Does the website have a blog?
- Is it immediately obvious, on every page of the site, what the business does and for whom?

In almost every marketing review that we carry out, we end up suggesting greater clarity in the text on the pages. Your visitors aren't familiar with your business and they're so distracted and busy that they don't have time to hunt around, trying to figure out if you might be a good fit for them. In digital marketing, clarity is a highly prized skill.

For some readers, this first step is a good time to make an important decision about the future of their website. If your website is not ranking, is a long way from being where it needs to be, and you have no control over improving it (or the person who does have control charges huge sums of money or takes ages), then this is the best time to get a website built that you *can* get into and make the necessary changes. It *can* be quicker (and sometimes even cheaper) to build a website from scratch than to negotiate with web designers who don't understand SEO, not to mention that an invisible website is costing you a lot *more* money in lost business than a highly-visible one would cost to be developed. Sometimes it's a hard decision, particularly if funds are tight or the previous developer is a close friend or family member. However, business is business, and, looking back, you'll see it as one of the best business decisions you made.

You know by now that we love WordPress and loads of the sites that Exposure Ninja builds for our clients are WordPress (unless the business suits Shopify better, which our team are great at building on too) because it gives you complete control over the content and structure in a simple and non-technical way. If you're technically competent, you might want to have a go at building your own WordPress site. We have some help available in the form of our video course *WordPress Mastery Made Simple*, which is included as part of our MarketingU video training over at www.marketingu.ninja.

Step 2: Keyword Targeting

Next, you want to identify the key phrases that you're going to be targeting. This keyword research should be linked closely to your competitor analysis, as your most successful competitors can be a rich source of target keywords. Spend some time searching using the phrases that your customers are most likely to search for and observe:

- Which are the keywords that your closest *business* competitors seem to be showing up for?
- How aggressively are they targeting these phrases? Which pages on their websites are showing up (i.e. is it a blog post? Product page? Service page? Their homepage?)
- How much text is on the pages that are ranking best?
- Are the keywords you're searching for included in the page titles and meta descriptions?
- How much text is on their pages?
- Are there lots of adverts showing up for these phrases? This can imply commercial intent and that there is profit to be made.
- Use a keyword tool and study the estimated search volume. If you could rank top, you might pick up 30-35%

of that traffic. What sort of impact would that have on your business and would it be worth the fight?

You'll want to go through the keyword research process outlined in Section 1 to draw up your list of target keywords. Be aware that you'll probably evolve these over time.

If you're already running a well-managed Google Ads campaign and you have data about the keywords that are generating the most conversions for you, this is really useful information to guide your SEO keyword research. We'll often run a PPC campaign in conjunction with an SEO campaign to get information about which phrases are proving to be most profitable, because they aren't always the phrases that have the highest search volume or the most competition.

Step 3: Competitor Analysis

Next, we want to size up your competition for each of these phrases. You'll usually find that it's the same group of sites showing up for a range of phrases so you might pick 5-10 sites that you want to focus on.

Get to know their websites well:

- Do they use different pages for each product or service or is everything on one page?
- How is the website structured?
  - o Are there a lot of pages all linked from the homepage or do you go through different levels of pages to find more and more specialised content?

    o Do they have pages at different levels (for example /shoes/womens/flat-shoes) or is everything on one level (for example /flat-shoes)?

- How popular are their social media channels? Don't just look at follower numbers; how much *engagement* are they getting?

- What do their meta descriptions, title tags and meta keywords (if any) say on their best ranking pages? Find these by right clicking on an empty area of the page and clicking 'View Source'

- How big is the site?

    o Are there a lot of pages?

    o Do they blog a lot? What sort of topics do they blog about?

- What does their link profile look like? Use Open Site Explorer, ahrefs or Semrush to see what sort of links they have. Have they been getting talked about on lots of websites and how high is the authority of these sites?

Just by spending time analysing and crawling through your most successful competitors, you'll start picking up ideas and building your own 'machine learning' awareness of what it takes to win in your market.

Step 4: Website Optimisation

The next step is to go a little bit deeper with your website's optimisation. This covers things like:

- Optimising your page titles and meta descriptions on every page.

- Increasing the amount of text copy and adding unique text copy to product pages.

- Making sure that your target keywords are in use throughout your website, particularly in page headings.

- Checking that those headings use the correct H1, H2 and H3 tags.

- Checking that you have a sitemap and that it's submitted through Google Search Console.

- Compressing website images using a plugin like Shortpixel.

- Installing caching and minification plugins to speed up your website, if necessary.

- Adding additional pages, if necessary, to target more competitive or commercial phrases.

Website optimisation is a never-ending process, particularly if you have a large website. As long as the main site pages are well optimised, it's okay to go back to product pages and less important pages later on to, for example, increase the amount of text copy on them. For instance, when we're working on a large eCommerce site, we'll add copy to a certain number of products per month once the main website optimisation has been handled and we're starting with the offsite promotion.

Step 5: Phase 1 Links

The first things to check are the basic links: your business directories, video websites and social media pages. These are quick to get set up or amended and, whilst they won't have you hitting top spot on their own, checking that they are all there is a good first step.

Step 6: Phase 2 Links

The second phase is when you'll start your content marketing. For most businesses, content marketing will form the bulk of the ongoing SEO work and is never 'finished' because there are always more publications and angles to target. It is this area in particular that even larger companies with dedicated marketing departments tend to look at outsourcing because the time and energy required to get enough exposure to dominate a competitive market is beyond their spare capacity. Whether you're a solopreneur or marketing manager, you likely don't have a spare 100 hours per month to run a content marketing campaign in addition to doing the other five full-time jobs you juggle!

Whether you take the DIY route or bring in outside help, the first step should always be topic research. We like to create a content calendar so we can begin to plan the article angles we'll be taking over the next 3-6 months, then plan blog posts and outreach around those.

Next, you'll want to start compiling a list of the websites that you'd like to discuss getting content published on. These might be blogs, magazine sites, news sites or industry-specific websites like trade journals, depending on your products and services. We'll put all of these contacts into a spreadsheet so that we can run the outreach in an organised way, and keep track of the people we've reached out to, the article ideas we've pitched and the results.

If you're not already blogging consistently, this is the time to start doing so. Remember that quality is more important than quantity, so if you get one or two detailed, long-form posts published on your site each month which begin to rank for commercial intent phrases, that's a great start.

Step 7: Measure Progress and Refocus

We'll look at how and what to track in the next chapter. Every three months, we do what we call a 'Quarterly Campaign Checkup', or QCC for short. The QCC is a chance to realign the SEO work with the goals of the business and it's something that you can do for yourself, too. If you're pushed for time, you can move these checkups to every six months. The important thing is that you don't become obsessed with 'ranking for ranking's sake'. Remember that everything we're doing in this book is designed to increase *leads* or *sales*, not just ranking. It's not uncommon for the results of such a checkup to be that we alter the keywords we're targeting, or recommend some tweaks to the website layout now that data has been collected about the site's performance.

To download the actual Quarterly Campaign Checkup framework that we use at Exposure Ninja to realign client campaigns, go to https://exposureninja.com/google-book, sign up for lifetime book updates, and I'll send it over.

Over time, it's natural that your SEO focus will change. Perhaps you'll add more products or services and these will have different keywords that you'd like to get ranking. You may start to dominate ranking for less competitive longer-tail phrases, giving you the confidence to move your focus to shorter-tail, higher volume and more competitive phrases. You might begin to hit saturation point for your main commercial phrases and decide to build a knowledge base on your website to attract traffic from the 'researchers' and people further up the funnel. All these types of revisions and reflections are encouraged, as very few SEO campaigns should ever stay 'static'.

CHAPTER 31

How to measure your progress

It's quiz time!

Question 1 of 1: The single most important success metric of any SEO campaign is what?

A. The number of keywords the site is ranking for

B. The number of relevant keywords the site is ranking for

C. The volume of organic traffic

D. The ranking increases of the target keywords

E. The number of leads and sales from organic traffic

F. Money

If you answered F, you're correct! You money-grabbing capitalist, you! SEO is a marketing activity, and the point of marketing is to sell stuff and make money. So, really, the only thing that is worth a damn in the long term is how much time or money you put into SEO and what you get out.

Now, before the entire SEO industry appears outside Ninja HQ with flaming torches, let me add an asterisk; whilst your website's ranking is increasing, there will be a period of time where the 'money' metric is not moving much or is going in the wrong direction. This is perfectly normal as there's a period of investment required to 'sow' authority and content before you start to 'reap' the increased ranking and financial rewards. So, if your friend is three months into SEO for their brand new website and complaining that they're not seeing a total return on their investment yet, have a quiet word. To add a second asterisk, the 'money' also depends on other non-SEO variables (website performance, sales process, product-market fit, etc.).

For this reason, all of the above metrics are useful in tracking the performance of an SEO campaign and we'll look at how to track each one in turn.

How to measure how many keywords your website is ranking for

The easiest way to do this is to go to a tool like Semrush, stick in your website's address, choose your target location and see how many keywords you're showing up for.

Go to https://thankyouninjas.com to get a 30-day free trial of Semrush, which you can use to check your ranking.

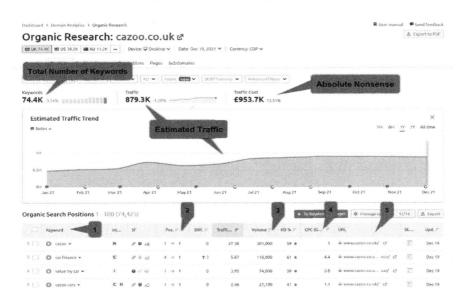

The text in the image is fairly small, but you can see that not only does Semrush show you how many keywords the website is ranking for; it also estimates how much traffic they are bringing in each month. It's important to remember that this is an *estimate*, based on the estimated search volume multiplied by the percentage of people that Semrush estimates would click on a website ranking in that position. Yes, the traffic number is two estimates multiplied together. The "traffic cost" then adds in a third estimate to guess how much this traffic would have cost were it picked up through PPC ads. An estimate multiplied by an estimate multiplied by an estimate. Ignore.

The table below the chart (with columns marked 1-5) sees a welcome return to fact. It shows each of the keywords indexed by Semrush which the website ranks for (column 1), the position on Google (2), an estimate of the monthly search volume (3), an estimate of how much people are willing to bid for Google Ads clicks for that keyword (4) and the particular page URL that is ranking (5).

How to measure and track the most relevant keywords

This overall ranking is a useful thing to keep an eye on but in amongst all the phrases you're ranking for there will be a lot of low commercial-intent rubbish that you have no intention of trying to rank for. For that reason, it's also useful to track the performance of your *target* keywords.

You can do this inside Semrush, or you can use other tools like https://seranking.com (which you can try for free by going to bestninjatool.com) or www.ranktracker.com, both of which are cheaper.

When you use a rank tracking tool like this, you'll first need to input all of the phrases that you want to track and choose your location. The tool will then measure your ranking for these phrases every day, giving you a day-by-day impression of your site's visibility. It can be tempting to become obsessed by your daily rankings and allow your mood to veer between elation and devastation depending on the direction of your rankings on a particular day. The truth is that rankings will fluctuate even as they increase over time.

To reassure you of this fact, I've copied below some client ranking charts from Semrush. These charts show how each website's visibility has changed over time and you'll notice on many that there have been periods of increase, decrease, and those frustrating flatlines which, at the time, feel like the end of the world. SEO, like market domination, is about the long game though. You can see on all of these that, by using the exact strategies in this book, all have seen significant long-term increases in their visibility. The pink arrows show when they started to take SEO seriously and follow the processes in this book (in this case, the pink arrows show when they started working with us but if you are going to be doing this DIY or working with your current agency, the same patterns apply, even if slightly slower).

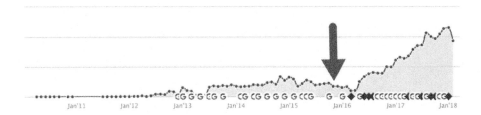

Notice how, in this example, rankings continued to *fall* almost immediately after starting SEO? Given the long-term picture, we can see that the impact of the new, well-optimised website we started building and that launched shortly after, will have a positive impact. At the time, though, was this scary for the business? You bet! Are they glad they stuck it out? You bet!

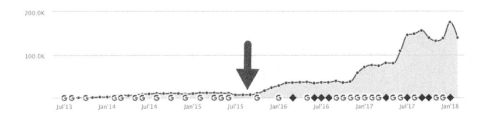

This is an example of a business lucky enough to see consistent growth throughout their SEO. Even so, there are periods of flatline performance—for almost the entire year in 2016, for example. This type of path is often due to not investing the time, energy or money into content marketing that's required to compete in the market. The site will reach its maximum ranking given its content and optimisation and further improvements require a different level of authority. We increased the level of content marketing, unlocked new levels of ranking and they are now in the top three in their highly competitive UK market.

Another example here shows vast improvement in the 3-4 month period, typical of website optimisation. Growth then remains flat, or even drops, before increasing significantly again once the content marketing work starts to take effect.

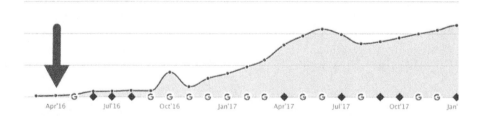

Imagine being this business in November 2016. You've been plugging away at SEO since April and things seemed to be improving, with organic visibility doubling within a couple of months. Then, last month (October 2016) you saw a huge increase. You're spending the Christmas money in your head already but when November's numbers come in, you're disappointed to see that almost all that increase is gone! Has Santa Google decided that you will only receive coal this year? Well, your Christmas 2017 looked *very* different indeed! Persistence rewarded!

I share these ranking graphs to give you hope on those long, lonely nights when you wonder if all of those blog posts, outreach emails, speed improvements and keywords have *really* been worth it. Trust me, if you follow the processes in this book, your business *will* see a significant benefit, whether it happens in two months, six months, or a year. The common thread amongst (almost) all of the examples here is that they saw *some* improvement fairly quickly. With the exception of the first site, which was experiencing a continued decline and continued to do so until we rebuilt the website, all of these cases saw enough improvement in the first 3-6 months to know that it was worth sticking with. All have been rewarded many times over for that patience and the impact of these types of ranking increases on the businesses behind the websites has been significant.

In many cases, the structure and 'behind the scenes' features of each of these businesses also needed to change. We've had clients go from a couple thousand dollars in sales per month to more than a million dollars and that requires some pretty significant process upgrades! Luckily, these happened gradually enough for their businesses not to immediately need to take on capital for stock, rush hiring decisions and have to scramble to keep up. They could grow consistently and rapidly but without overstretching and risking their stability.

Remember that I and the Exposure Ninja team are always here to offer a second opinion on your ranking growth. Feel free to email us at googlebook@exposureninja.com if you're concerned that things have stalled and you want some advice on what to do next.

The free website and marketing review at https://exposure ninja.com/google-book also gets another mention, as it really is a fantastic resource.

CHAPTER 32

Outsourcing vs DIY

One of the biggest decisions you have to make about the future digital marketing growth of your business is if, how, and when to outsource some or all of this work. The first thing I will say is that there are examples in almost every market where the business has generated huge growth by doing this in-house. Despite running an SEO company, my advice to you is not YOU SHOULD ALWAYS OUTSOURCE YOUR SEO.

My second piece of advice is this; even if you decide to out-source some or all of your SEO, don't abdicate completely. You need to understand at least the basics of what your SEO company is doing for you and you need to monitor their work enough to know whether you're getting good work for the money. Just as you wouldn't bury your head in the sand and leave the finances of the business to go totally unchecked, you should not stop taking notice of your marketing company's activity. Both have the potential to impact your business positively or negatively, so ignoring it is not a viable option.

My third piece of advice is that if you *do* decide to outsource, don't underestimate the value that you bring. For example, we have a large team of Content Marketing Ninjas at Exposure

Ninja who spend their lives researching and writing blogs and articles to become world class experts on their topics, so they are excellent at doing this. However, none of them know as much about your business as you. None of them know the ins and outs, the trends, or have predictions for the future of your industry, products and services like you do. Your expertise and knowledge should be tightly integrated into any marketing plan, so don't fall into the all-too-easy trap of thinking that SEO is purely technical geekery. Yes, there's a lot of that, but it's also about amplifying your voice online. A great SEO company will do that but there has to be a voice to amplify!

Here are some questions to ask if you're weighing up outsourcing your SEO or doing it yourself:

- Are you or your team pressured for time? You will typically need to dedicate at least 10 hours per week to SEO if you plan to do it yourself. If you're in a competitive or well-established market, this could rise to 25-50 if you're planning to do content marketing as well.

- Do you enjoy both technical and creative tasks or does your team have a mixture of these skills? SEO requires both technical (analysis of keywords and search volumes, optimisation of websites, etc.) and creative (content marketing, blog writing, planning outreach campaigns, etc.) tasks. One without the other will lead to results plateauing. We usually have a minimum of three people with complementary skillsets working on each SEO campaign for this exact reason, so whilst it's definitely possible to handle the whole thing yourself, you might find it easier (and more fun) if you have at least one other well chosen person to balance out your skills.

- Do you have a source of funding? This can be either sales or startup investment. Outsourcing SEO requires a period of investment before it pays for itself. If you only have the budget for 1-2 months of SEO work, it might make more sense to keep it in-house, as very few companies will be able to bring significant improvement in that sort of timescale.

My final piece of advice is that just because you *can* do something yourself, doesn't mean you *should*. Without fail, every single one of our most financially successful clients is extremely protective over their time and don't take on anything that they can have someone else do for them, whether it's us handling their SEO or their team handling day-to-day elements of their business. They recognise their unique talents and reserve their time and energy to do the things that only they can do.

Having said that, they *all* take a keen interest in the work they pay us to do.

CHAPTER 33

Further help and advice

I hope that this book has given you the information you need to transform the impact that your website has on your business because that's all any of this is about, really. Hopefully you can see that, while it's not *easy* to rank number one (and some markets are certainly tougher than others), the tasks involved are actually relatively simple. It all really comes down to building a readable website, making it useful to people and then promoting it like a Ninja.

If, having seen what is involved in getting a website to the top of Google, you have decided that you would like some help with some or all of your SEO work, then we'd love to talk with you about taking it on, so you can get on with running your business. Exposure Ninja builds websites and provides SEO and online promotion for businesses, whether local, national or international. We're good at what we do and genuinely offer a level of promotion work that is unheard of at our price point.

If you have any questions about anything in this book, or find anything that you're unsure about or need help with, feel free to reach out to me personally at googlebook@exposure ninja.com.

Even if you're not ready to have Exposure Ninja handle your marketing, we can still help you. Collectively, the Ninjas spend thousands of hours a week doing digital marketing for our clients and we share everything we learn and develop to help others. A lot of this information finds its way into the training section on our website. Go to https://exposureninja.com/training to see our range of free training and webinars. Everything we do is in plain English and designed to help you *succeed*, not just 'buy our stuff'.

If videos are your thing, you should definitely subscribe to our YouTube channel (which just passed 1,000,000 views).

I publish at least one video a week, but most weeks, there are two. I publish instructional videos on how you can improve your website and marketing, as well as publish digital marketing strategy analysis of successful businesses in all kinds of industries. Here are a few of the most popular ones:

Learn Digital Marketing

- How To Write Perfect Page Titles and Meta Descriptions for SEO

  (https://youtu.be/rzxnwSR3i8A)

- How To Find Your Target Audience in 6 Questions

  (https://youtu.be/t0meZUDSJv4)

- How To Get To The Top of Google

  (https://youtu.be/Cti-BUkCFZI)

- How To Create Landing Pages That Convert at 43%

  (https://youtu.be/jR7z2ph4DrA)

- How to Choose the Right Keywords for SEO

  (https://youtu.be/_2eAXgvFOkg)

- 6 Tips to Increase Your eCommerce Sales

  (https://youtu.be/GFA2xyyMRgQ)

- How To Reach 100 Sales a Day on Your Website

  (https://youtu.be/g5pHYRJxF0E)

- How To Optimise Your Website For Core Web Vitals

  (https://youtu.be/JG3fQZKv3n0)

- Secrets of 3 Successful Shopify Marketing Strategies

  (https://youtu.be/25TV2T3fIss)

- 15 Fast Ways to Increase Your eCommerce Sales

  (https://youtu.be/LWCEsb7t8fs)

Marketing Strategy Analysis

- Gymshark's Marketing Strategy

  (https://youtu.be/uQ_rAb2qTNQ)

- The Hut Group's Marketing Strategy

  (https://youtu.be/cP53msdmAYA)

- Peloton's Marketing Strategy

  (https://youtu.be/x0yCG1w7Np4)

- Boohoo's Marketing Strategy

  (https://youtu.be/6tVwQmVFfM0)

- Huel's Marketing Strategy

  (https://youtu.be/wv47DdGdJQc)

- Monday.com's Marketing Strategy

  (https://youtu.be/3CCt4jpnB3k)

If you're a podcast person, you might like to check out the Exposure Ninja Digital Marketing Podcast (https://link. chtbl.com/googlebook), which I host every week (search for "Exposure Ninja" in your favourite podcast player). You'll hear me explain how you can use digital marketing to increase your revenue (using the same processes we use for our clients), as well as look at successful digital marketing campaigns from the business world and how they did it.

Here are some must-listen episodes:

- How To Create Landing Pages That Convert at 43%

  (https://exposureninja.com/podcast/174)

- How To Create a Winning Marketing Strategy in 5 Steps

  (https://exposureninja.com/podcast/169)

- How to Write Blogs That Rank Top of Google

  (https://exposureninja.com/podcast/183)

- How To Create The Perfect Website Sales Funnel

  (https://exposureninja.com/podcast/182)

- 3 Content Marketing Steps to CRUSH Your Competitors With Killer Content

  (https://exposureninja.com/podcast/208)

- 5 Tips for Writing Blog Posts That Generate Leads

  (https://exposureninja.com/podcast/196)

- How To Write Compelling Website Copy That Sells

  (https://exposureninja.com/podcast/175)

If you're planning to do your own marketing due to budget constraints, then we've built a DIY marketing training website called MarketingU (www.marketingu.ninja), especially for you.

This is the 'secret lair' where we share video tutorials showing exactly how to use the marketing strategies that our clients pay us thousands for. Designed for DIY digital marketers, the videos inside MarketingU show you step-by-step, how to market your business online using a range of marketing channels, from PPC to Facebook ads, social media management to email marketing and, of course, SEO. It's a fantastic resource if you're planning to 'go it alone' but want to save yourself the inevitable experimenting time and just copy what works. If you've found this book useful, you'll *love* MarketingU.

Use the voucher code ILOVETIM to get a discount on membership, and I'll see you on the inside.

You can get access to our digital marketing strategy and priority system too. We call it the 90-Minute Marketing Masterplan. It's a video course spread over five days that'll help you to put all of your marketing tasks into a revenue-focused priority order—and you can get it for free by going to https://exposureninja.com/90.

And if you haven't gotten them already, you can download all the spreadsheets I've mentioned within this book, plus several **must have** checklists too, by going to https://exposureninja.com/google-book-freebies. They're based on the same spreadsheets we use for our award-winning client campaigns, so you don't want to miss them.

Finally, in case you haven't noticed, Exposure Ninja offers a free website and marketing review, which is the perfect first step if you want to improve the sales that your website generates. We've covered a lot in this book and SEO is only one piece of the digital marketing puzzle, so the free review is a great way to get a prioritised action plan that you can follow in order to increase your website's visibility and sales. If you'd like to work with Exposure Ninja, the free review is also the first step to doing this. Go to https://exposureninja.com/google-book to request yours now.

Before You Go...

I'm lucky enough to have met hundreds of people at various events and expos over the years since I published the first edition of this book in 2013.

It's been wonderful to hear the stories of business owners and marketers who've done incredible things with their websites after having read this book, some of whom became our earliest clients, of which a few are still with us today. It fills me with a lot of pride.

Unfortunately, I've yet to meet all of the thousands of people who've read this book to hear how it's affected their lives and their websites.

The next best thing, however, is the reviews the book receives on Amazon (nine years later and I still read them all).

Please, if you get a moment, leave an honest review of this book on Amazon. Obviously, I'm only human, and I'd love for you to leave a glowing review, but what I really care most about is that you're truthful.

If you didn't like the book, do say so. If there's something that could be better, include that in your review. But if you enjoyed it, maybe learned something from it too, please let me know. It means a lot to me and the Ninjas who help keep this book updated and relevant every year.

Thank you.

P.S. If you REALLY love it, then be sure to check out our other books:

- Profitable Social Media Marketing: How To Grow Your Business Using Facebook, Twitter, Instagram, LinkedIn and More

    (amzn.to/3H3xk1Q)

- The Ultimate Guide To Content Marketing & Digital PR

    (amzn.to/3J2OUoG)

- 101 Ways To Get More Customers From The Internet

    (amzn.to/3sjkpoF)

Printed in Great Britain
by Amazon

83480423R00173